THE NEXT STEP

A Catholic Teen's Guide to Surviving High School

BY RACHEL ALLEN

EDGE LIFE TEEN

Unless otherwise noted, Scripture passages have been taken from the Revised Standard Version, Catholic edition. Copyright ©1946, 1952, 1971 by the Division of Christian Education of the National Council of the Churches of Christ in the USA. Used by permission. All rights reserved.

Quotes are taken from the English translation of the Catechism of the Catholic Church for the United States of America (indicated as CCC), 2nd ed. Copyright ©1997 by United States Catholic Conference – Libreria Editrice Vaticana.

©2014 Life Teen, Inc. All rights reserved. No part of this book, including interior design, cover design, and/or icons, may be reproduced or transmitted in any form, by any means (electronic, photocopying, recording, or otherwise) without prior written permission from the publisher.

The views and opinions expressed within this work are those of the author and do not necessarily reflect the views of Life Teen.

The information contained herein is published and produced by Life Teen, Inc. The resources and practices are in full accordance with the Roman Catholic Church. The Life Teen® name and associated logos are trademarks registered with the United States Patent and Trademark Office. Use of the Life Teen® trademarks without prior permission is forbidden. Permission may be requested by contacting Life Teen, Inc. at 480-820-7001.

Designed by Casey Olson.

Authored by Rachel Allen.

Copy editing by Natalie Tansill, Christina Mead, and Rachel Peñate.

ISBN: 978-0-9915965-2-2

Copyright ©2014 Life Teen, Inc. All rights reserved.

Published by Life Teen, Inc.
2222 S. Dobson Rd.
Suite 601
Mesa, AZ 85202

LifeTeen.com
Printed in the United States of America.
Printed on acid-free paper.

For more information about Life Teen or to order additional copies, go online to LifeTeen.com or call us at 1-800-809-3902.

TABLE // OF // CONTENTS

INTRODUCTION
Not Missing Middle School... At All - v

PART // ONE
How-To's for High School

// **ONE** // Making The Grade: Academics - 3

// **TWO** // Extra, Extra: Extracurricular Activities - 9

// **THREE** // Social Skills: Navigating Social Media And More - 15

PART // TWO
Relationships

// **FOUR** // Relationship Status? It's Complicated: Family - 27

// **FIVE** // Best Friends Forever?: Friendship - 35

// **SIX** // The First Time I Fell In Love: God - 43

PART // THREE
Chastity

// SEVEN // What Does That Word Even Mean?!: Introduction - 55

// EIGHT // Don't Waste Your First Kiss: Dating - 63

// NINE // Media Savvy: Purity of Mind - 71

EPILOGUE
Don't Worry About High School — Jesus Doesn't - 79

//INTRODUCTION//
Not Missing Middle School... At All

I've gone to Catholic schools my whole life. Moving on from my Catholic middle school to a Catholic co-ed high school, I graduated from eighth grade with about 60 other kids. I had a core group of six girls that were my best friends, but none of us went on to high school together. And I hated... *hated* middle school.

It's not that my middle school was a bad place. It was actually a pretty good place, with teachers who cared and priests who worked hard to engage us in our faith. My classmates were (mostly) really nice kids, and we didn't have a lot of drama. But my fondest middle school memories definitely come from graduating and moving on.

I have a confession to make — the reason I didn't like junior high is mostly because I didn't like me. I was an awkward middle school kid. I was a smart kid but not an athletic one, and I didn't like the way I looked. I had glasses and crooked teeth (and didn't get braces to fix them until I was a senior in high school), and I definitely thought I weighed too much. I had crushes on guys who didn't want to talk to me. I wasn't part of the popular group. My best friends were awesome, but we kept to ourselves a lot and it felt like the rest of our class never really noticed us. There were a lot of times when I felt invisible. And it's not like I had a relationship with God to help me get through it. I only went to church because I had to.

So when I graduated from middle school, it was "good riddance and nice knowing ya!" I couldn't wait to take the next step — to walk through the doors of my high school and start fresh. I wanted new people who didn't know me yet. I wanted to be someone other than all the labels I had before. I was ready to go.

But I know that isn't everyone's middle school experience. For some of you, junior high has been awesome. Maybe you've been with the same friends since kindergarten and your relationships are rock-solid. Maybe you've had a lot of success in school, sports, and other activities. Maybe you're even going on to high school with all the same kids you've known your whole life. High school will be a lot of the same stuff, just in a different building.

But whether your middle school experience has been awesome or awful, the reality is that it's over. You did it. It's time to get on with it and move forward to the next step. You're going from the top of the totem pole to the bottom of the pile, and high school (even if it's with all of the same people) is going to be a brand new experience. And if you want, you can be someone new, too.

I may not actually know you, but I definitely do care about you. And this book is for you — to help you figure out everything that comes with the high school experience: grades, sports, clubs, family, friends, dating, social media, God... we're going to talk about it all.

I hope it will be helpful to you — because I think you're really awesome. I love your sense of humor, and I really care about what's going on in your life. Although I don't actually know you, I do want high school to be an amazing place for you, where you can become the person God created you to be.

Because as much as I hated middle school, I loved high school. I'm praying that you'll love it, too, and I'm here to help you handle it. Because high school... it's happening. So, here's how to take the next step.

PART // ONE

How-To's for High School

// ONE //

MAKING THE GRADE: ACADEMICS

First things first: As you take this next step into high school, it's important to realize that you're going to... well... school. And while the classroom may not be your favorite place on campus, it is the most important room you'll step into. It's the main reason you're even in the building. Your classes (and grades and tests and homework) are about to take over a huge portion of your life — so get ready.

I have always been one of those "smart kids." You know the type. Actually enjoyed reading, always knew the answers in class, never did well in gym. Hey, there's no shame in that. I think we'd all agree that it's helpful to get good grades and do well in school. Being a smart kid is a good thing — but let's be honest: in middle school, I hated that label.

Because, while no one is ever going to be upset about having a brain that works well or wish that they were dumber, we also know that being smart can be kind of dangerous for your reputation. When I was in middle school, there were kids in my class who were only my friends on group project days because they knew that if I was in their group, it would help jack up their grade.

But then, they never seemed to want to hang out on the weekends. Maybe they thought I was too busy, sitting at home alone, reading Wikipedia? I didn't do that. If you do, it's cool. But I didn't. And I hated the way my classmates used me for my brain in class and ignored me the rest of the time.

So when I got to high school, I decided to keep my "smart kid" status on the down low as long as humanly possible. I didn't want to get stuck in that same box again. And that started with the very first assignment in Freshman Bio, during my first week of high school.

> "Pray as if everything depended on God and work as if everything depended on you" (attributed to St. Ignatius of Loyola).

We were learning the names of the bones. Our teacher had a model skeleton at the front of the classroom, and she rattled off all the bones as we filled in the blanks on worksheets at our desks. She told us that by the end of the week, there would be a quiz — so get to memorizing.

Later that week, she wheeled that same skeleton out in front of her desk and asked if anyone could name all the bones for the class. Crickets chirped for a few minutes, and my heart was racing. I knew I could do it. But I also didn't want to be labeled as a smart kid, again. So, I just sat there, with the rest of my classmates, and waited.

Maybe a minute later (although it obviously felt like an eternity), a guy named Ben raised his hand. Ben was a really good athlete and a genuinely nice guy. He'd come to our high school from one of the local Catholic middle schools with a few other kids and seemed to already have a place where he fit in. He was playing football and was comfortable in his classes and had every reason in the world to be confident.

And there, in front of all of us, he named every bone in the human body. When he finished, our teacher made a little speech that I still can't forget. She said that Ben was a leader. She talked about the courage it took for Ben to put himself out there like that, and how, even if Ben hadn't gotten all the bones right, he had set the bar for the rest of us. But he had gotten all the bones right, on top of it all. He had become one of the first leaders of our freshman class, right in front of our eyes.

… and I felt *stupid* for sitting quietly in my seat when I could have done exactly what he just did.

Because I wanted to be a leader, too. I knew I had what it took. I could have named all those bones — but more than that, I wanted to be *seen*. I remembered all those times in middle school when I felt invisible and I really hoped that high school would be different — a place where I could be more confident in who I was and what I could do.

But... I also didn't want to be seen in the wrong light. I wanted to stand out for something other than just being smart. I hadn't seen naming the bones as a leadership opportunity, so I stayed quiet. And in that moment, my first chance to be somebody, I let Ben do what I couldn't do.

Now, it seems kind of silly that I didn't speak up in that moment, because the reality is that we can't hide who we are forever. Word got out — I was a smart kid. I was in the advanced classes and made good grades. No one was ever going to confuse me with one of the kids who struggled in school.

"Since we have gifts that differ according to the grace given to us, let us exercise them" (Romans 12:6).

But as much as that moment in Freshman Bio was about being a leader, it was also about what we were learning in school. We had been given an assignment to memorize the bones. And I had done it, and done it well (although don't ask me to rattle them off now). Look, guys: being the "smart kid" isn't a liability. It's a gift — and in that moment, I had wasted that gift. The part that bothered me the most was that I didn't step up to the plate when I *knew* I could play the game. I had the goods. I was smart enough to make it happen, and I didn't.

Whether we like it or not, academics are a major part of high school. From day one, college counselors come into freshmen classrooms and start talking about admissions essays and GPAs — I'm pretty sure I first heard those words during our freshman orientation. Your class schedule, test scores, and grades will have a major impact

"Well done, My good and faithful servant. Since you were faithful in small matters, I will give you great responsibilities. Come, share your Master's joy" (Matthew 25:23).

on your future. And your high school teachers are going to push you a lot harder than your teachers did in junior high.

For some of you, it's easy to make the grade. In middle school, you pulled off A's and B's without really trying. But the time has come when that isn't going to cut it — you're going to have to work at it now, when you didn't have to before. And for others, it's a lot tougher — you have to bust your butt to pull off a C-average. There are some subjects you really like and others where you struggle. Some teachers teach in a style that works for you, while others might as well be speaking a foreign language (... and some are actually speaking a foreign language, but that's just because they're trying to teach it to you).

But no matter what the classroom was like for you in junior high, your high school classroom is a fresh start. Your classes will be what you make of them, and I hope you won't make any excuses. Don't let a bad teacher, a boring subject, or a middle school label (whether that's "smart kid" or "struggles in school") define your high school academic career.

You will start over in high school. The slate is clean. And you have what it takes to get the most out of your classes. You can choose to slack off or study hard. Right now, your main job is your schoolwork, so give it everything you've got.

And if you do, I bet you'll find the subject where you really connect. We all have different interests, different gifts, and talents, and I promise you that there is a classroom in your high school where you were created to be. You know what I'm talking about? That place where things just make sense. It might be math, art, woodshop, whatever. I could do chemistry and math, with a little extra effort, but I definitely didn't prefer them. I would have much rather spent all day in a Literature class because that was where I *belonged*. It was a place where I thrived, a place where I grew more and more into the person that God created me to be.

I don't know what gifts God has given you, but I promise that even if they aren't exactly academic, there will be a place in your high school where you will be able to use them. And even if academics are the place where you have to work the hardest — do the work. The school part may not be your favorite aspect of high school (awkward, but true for some of us), but it's incredibly important. And putting the work into it is worth it.

After high school, you may go to college, and then graduate school, or law school, or medical school… you might be in school for the next ten years of your life, or longer. Maybe that sounds exciting, or maybe it sounds like torture. I'm sure that it sounds like it's forever away, but it might be the road you take. And if that's the path you're heading down, you'll want to do your best to get into good habits now. It's a lot easier to maintain good study habits from the beginning than it is to build them up later.

> "Let us not grow tired of doing good, for in due time, we shall reap our harvest, if we do not give up" (Galatians 6:9).

Or high school might be the last chance you'll ever have to be a student. You could walk off the stage with your high school diploma into a job and you might never look back. You might spend the rest of your life at a desk in a cubicle. The time you have in a classroom, it's a gift — maybe not a gift you asked for or even want, but definitely a gift. I understand the temptation to blow it off or get lazy, but don't. Give it your very best because it may be the last chance you have to enjoy it.

I hope that while you're in high school, you'll work hard on your academics. You decide, on day one, how much effort you're going to put into it. There are going to be plenty of distractions coming your way over the next four years. So many things will try and pull your focus from your real high school career — being a student.

> "Ordinary work, which is what most of us do most of the time, is ordained by God every bit as much as is the extraordinary" (Elisabeth Elliot, *The Shaping of a Christian Family*).

Use your classes to stand out as a leader. Use them to turn over a new leaf. Use them to find out what you're really passionate about. Use your classes to set yourself up for future successes. I don't care how you use them, just use them — because how hard you work in your classes now will have a huge effect on your future life.

And know that God is trying to use you — your brain, your gifts, and your talents — for His glory. So let Him.

// TWO //

Extra, Extra: Extracurricular Activities

All right, now that we've covered all of that "pay attention in class; your grades are important" stuff (but don't forget about it — we talked about it first because it's *so* important!), let's move on to the rest of the high school experience. Academics are a huge part of high school, but let's be serious: there are other, much more interesting things to focus on, right? (Settle down, I'm not talking about the opposite sex; don't worry, we'll get to that later.)

I'm sure you've known which sports you want to play in high school long before you've known your class schedule. You're probably even going out for a few before the first day of school. Football camps start in August, right? And so do cheer camps, theater camps, and every other kind of camp under the sun.

> "We were sent into the world by God, just as Jesus was. Once we start living our lives with that conviction, we will soon know what we were sent to do"
> (Henri Nouwen, *Bread for the Journey*).

Yes, it is totally awesome that there are so many opportunities to go out for different activities in high school. High school has tons of options when it comes to your free time and I hope you'll have more to say at the end of your high school career than, "Well, I watched a lot of Netflix."

But before you dive into any (or all) of them, take a second and think carefully — what extracurricular activities are you going out for, and why?

First, I have to ask: Are you pursuing the stuff you're actually interested in? You know, the things that *you* really love, not just the things other people think you should love?

Maybe your parents, older siblings, or best friends are all about a certain activity, and you could either take it or leave it. But because they're all so passionate about it, you find yourself spending more and more time running laps around the track than building robots in your basement. I hope their expectations for you won't determine how you spend your time — whether that means getting into stuff you don't really care about, or avoiding things you love because someone else doesn't think it's cool.

Once, I met an eighth grade guy who told me that he loved the theater. He thought plays and musicals were so cool. He loved the music, the acting, the sets — everything about it. He was probably such a big fan of the theater because his mom was a drama teacher at a local high school, and he had grown up going to see her productions.

But he shared with a small group of his classmates that he had asked his mom to "make him go" to see her shows... because he had a dad and big brother who were really into sports. He was afraid that if they knew how much he liked the theater, they would make fun of him.

So here's this kid who is totally passionate about something that's awesome, and yet because other people didn't think it was manly or cool, he hid his interest. That's no way to approach your passions.

But you know what was so cool about this guy sharing that with a small group of his buddies? After he said how hard it was to admit to anyone that he really liked theater, another guy in the group said, "I know what you mean. I think figure skating is so cool. But no one else does. So I've never told anyone how much I like it."

When you're able to be yourself, you give other people the courage to do the same. There's no right and wrong when it comes to your interests. They are *your* interests, and if you like them, you like them, and that's amazing. Don't let what other people think stop you from pursuing the things you that love. All the unique things you are into are what make you who you are.

It reminds me of this guy who once had the courage to go out for the school play, even though it went against what was considered cool. He was the star basketball player, after all, not a theater guy. And when people found out that he was trying something new, they all flipped out and told him, "If you want to be cool, follow one simple rule: Don't mess with the flow, no no! Stick to the status quo." (Okay, okay, busted, I know… that happened in the movie *High School Musical*. But hey, it happens in real life, too!)

> "And whatever you do, in word or in deed, do everything in the name of the Lord Jesus, giving thanks to God the Father through Him" (Colossians 3:17).

What a bunch of garbage. Seriously?! If we all just stuck to what was expected of us, we'd never try anything new and we'd totally miss out on all the opportunities that are before us. In high school, you are going to have a LOT of options. Don't pass one up because you're worried about what other people think. What are the things you really love to do?

My freshman year, I wanted to try a few new things while still going out for the stuff that I already knew I loved. One of the things I got involved in right away at my school was our campus ministry. We had a group that did some of the "churchy" things around school, like help to plan the Masses and do some service work around town.

It was cool… but I wanted it to be better. My friend Jamie and I thought there should be more on campus about the pro-life movement. While there was a campus ministry group, there wasn't a specific pro-life club, so Jamie and I started one our junior year. We planned meetings, activities, and events (like a pilgrimage to Washington, D.C. in January for the annual March for Life), and we even trained the underclassmen so that they could keep the group going after we graduated.

If there's some group or club that you think is missing from your school, then start it. Why not?! There are always options for trying something new — maybe it's new to the school or just something new to you.

Like that stretch for a few months during my freshman year, where the thing to do after school was to sit around and play chess. I'd never played chess before in my life. But, I decided, why not give it a shot? Especially since one of the cutest guys in my class, who was waiting around after school before football practice started, was playing, too. But even though we didn't fall in love (probably because I started kicking his butt in chess and he didn't like to lose), I picked up a new skill. Turns out, I was pretty good at it.

> "WE CAN'T TAKE ANY CREDIT FOR OUR TALENTS. IT'S HOW WE USE THEM THAT COUNTS" (MADELEINE L'ENGLE, A WRINKLE IN TIME).

And don't worry if there are things going on that you're *not* good at and would rather avoid. I know myself — I'm not very athletic (not to stereotype, but remember that whole "smart kid" thing? Yeah, running makes me cry), so I didn't play any sports in high school. That might sound like a tragedy… but it isn't. Maybe there's a sport you'd love to play or a part in the musical that you think you're perfect for — and after the tryouts, someone else made the cut and you didn't.

I know how disappointing that can be, but I hope that if that happens to you, you won't let it turn your world upside down. There are plenty of other options, so trust that if God closes one door, He opens another window somewhere. Even though I'm not an athlete, I'm an awesome sports fan (remember the cute boy who played chess? I somehow managed to make it to all of his football games…), and I had a ton of fun cheering on my friends and classmates. Plus, not playing sports gave me time to pursue other activities where I was much more talented — and I made friends on the newspaper staff and in the theater that I never would have met on the soccer field.

Don't forget about the options outside of school, either. My number one priority, all four years of high school, was youth group. My parish youth ministry met on Wednesday and Sunday nights, so when I was checking out extracurriculars at school, I made sure that their schedules didn't overlap with youth group. It meant passing up the spring musical so I wouldn't miss every youth group meeting for two months each year. But it didn't mean skipping the fall play because those rehearsals didn't clash. I found those activities that worked with my priorities — and trust me, it's okay to not be a part of *everything*. Pick and choose wisely.

If you're going to a public high school, there may not be as many opportunities to feed your faith on campus. You probably won't have a campus ministry program, after all. So don't forget about youth ministry as an option, and look for other ways to bring faith into your school. For example, many high schools have chapters of FCA, the Fellowship of Christian Athletes. That can be a great way to combine two of your passions. If there isn't a chapter at your school... just start one.

> "IF WE LIVE THE FAITH IN OUR DAILY LIFE, THEN OUR WORK TOO BECOMES A CHANCE TO SPREAD THE JOY OF BEING A CHRISTIAN" (POPE FRANCIS).

And remember — no extracurricular activity defines you. I don't care if you're the quarterback, or the lead in the musical, or the editor-in-chief of your school newspaper. I don't care if you don't belong to a single group on campus. Either way, you aren't made up of the activities you love. You're made up of you. And if you start living your life for these activities, they'll take over in no time.

One of my best girlfriends in high school fell into that trap. She was a dancer and made our school's dance team right away as a freshman. She was at dance practice every day after school and worked every dance camp all summer. It's good to be dedicated to your passions, but she took it too far. She let that pressure to have the perfect dancer's body take over, and listened too closely to other people's comments about her weight — even though she was never actually overweight. It started a huge battle with food that she is still fighting today. No extracurricular is worth that kind of pain. Keep a healthy perspective — enjoy your passions, and don't let them take over your life.

Take your time, too. You don't need to start up ten new hobbies right away. Check out what's in place and feel it out. If you join every club on campus, and start five more while you're at it, you'll burn out in no time. Remember, school is your full-time job. Your classes have to come first, and the extras should be just that — extras.

> "IF YOU WISH TO GO TO EXTREMES, LET IT BE IN SWEETNESS, PATIENCE, HUMILITY, AND CHARITY" (ST. PHILIP NERI, ST. PHILIP NERI AND THE ROMAN SOCIETY OF HIS TIMES).

It's great to be involved in a bunch of activities because they'll help you be a well-rounded person. But the key is to be... well... *well-rounded*. Don't let anything become your number one. Only God can be your number one, and getting obsessed with anything else is a recipe for disaster.

It's so sweet that God is creative enough to give us all different gifts and talents — and I hope that you'll put yours to work in high school. Follow your passions and allow them to help you meet new people and maybe even make a difference on your campus. Don't worry about how anyone else thinks you should spend your time. If you pursue the things you love, it will make your high school experience the best it can possibly be.

// THREE //

Social Skills: Navigating Social Media and More

Recently, I was sitting at a lunch table with a group of junior high girls and we couldn't think of which actor was in what movie with which actress and when. The best way to settle the question, naturally, was to pull out our smartphones. But then the girls remembered that they weren't allowed to use their phones, since it was a school day. So they immediately turned to me, since I'm kind of a grown-up and those rules didn't apply to me.

I pulled my phone out of my pocket, and they started asking me which version it was, what apps I had, and where I got my phone case. They wanted every detail and started to make comparisons to their own phones, apps, and cases. It turned out that we had a lot in common when it came to technology — which just made me laugh because some of these girls had their phones for years, and when I was in middle school we didn't have anything like that. And I wasn't in middle school *that* long ago.

That's the thing, when it comes to technology: It changes so quickly. I could write a chapter about Facebook, and Twitter, and Vine, and Snapchat, and Instagram... and maybe none of those things will even be cool by the time you read this book (and it's OK if you don't know what any of those are. Just Google them and learn about the good ol' days. You guys still use Google... right?).

The social media turnover rate is so rapid. Technology is constantly changing. Remember when Instagram was just pictures, and then they added the ability to make videos? Who knows what they'll have added by the time you read this chapter… or if Instagram will still be a thing by then! One day it's in, and the next minute it's out.

And here's the biggest struggle when it comes to technology: With how quickly it all changes, there isn't really anyone who can teach you how to navigate it. You sort of have to figure it out on your own, which is incredibly challenging. Yes, obviously, you hear about the latest app from your friends and they show you how it works, but that's not exactly what I mean when it comes to navigating it…

Think about it this way: In a couple of years, you might learn how to drive. And chances are good that your parents will be the people who teach you how. I was taught to drive by both of my parents, and they had two very, very different teaching styles. My mom would tell me what to do and then let me do it… and then spend the rest of the time holding on to the door handle and pushing invisible brakes on her side of the vehicle. And no matter how many times I reminded her that there weren't any brakes on her side of the car, she'd still keep trying to hit them when she thought that I was going too fast.

My dad was a little more laid back, but he had his quirks, too. He'd tell me to turn left ahead, and then advise me when I should start slowing down in order to turn left ahead, and then let me know when it was a good time to hit my turn signal to let other drivers know that I was going to turn left ahead, *and then* tell me when to start hitting my gas in the middle of the left turn in order to maintain a good speed after I was finished making the left turn, and THEN talk for the next ten minutes about left turns and right turns and so on and so forth. No offense to my dad, but eventually I learned how to tune him out in the car. Let's be honest: Making a left turn wasn't THAT complicated. I didn't need a ten-minute explanation on how and why to do it.

Driving is such a big responsibility, and it can be a really dangerous thing if you don't know what you're doing. One mistake, one split-second of poor decision-making, and your whole life can change. And as much as I hated how my dad explained the same thing to me five different times in ten different ways, and as annoying as I thought it was when my mom hit her "air-brakes," in the end, I'm really glad that they took the time to teach me how to drive. I learned a lot from both of them, and I really love driving. It's a great thing to be able to go wherever I want, whenever I want to, and not depend on someone else for a ride. Driving myself around is a great freedom — and a huge responsibility.

And it was much, much better that I learned how to drive from my parents than from, say, my friends who'd only had their licenses for a month. My parents had been driving for a really long time and had so much experience on the roads. And they're two people who really love and care about me and want me to be safe. Their main interest was teaching me to drive in an environment where I'd be protected; we started on empty parking lots before we went on highways because they wanted to make sure that no one would get hurt as I learned this new skill.

> "With great power comes great responsibility" (Uncle Ben, Spider-Man (2002)).

And that's why I feel for you when it comes to social media: because NO ONE has skills or experience when it comes to navigating it, so no one can really walk you through it and teach you how it's done safely. We're all learning about it, together. As soon as a new technology comes out, we can find a million ways to use it for good — and the same number of ways to use it for evil.

Please don't think that I'm hating on technology. I love my smartphone and all the fun ways it connects me to my friends and family and the outside world as a whole. But I also know that using that technology is a great freedom (not a right) and a huge responsibility. One wrong move, one split-second of poor decision making, and I could really hurt myself and other people.

Here's the good news, though: Even if no one has a ton of experience on these technological roads, there are people in your life who have wisdom that can be applied to all kinds of situations.

You're probably already navigating this stuff, on some level. Even if you're not in on it yet, you probably will be soon. I know some teens your age who always have the latest iPhone, and some whose parents won't let them on any social

> "If any of you lacks wisdom, he should ask God who gives to all generously and ungrudgingly, and he will be given it" (James 1:5).

networking sites until they get into high school, at least. Even if you're not in on it yet, you probably will be soon. If you don't have an iPod Touch or a smartphone or a Twitter handle, I know some of your friends do. I bet your older siblings do. Maybe your parents even have them, too. You probably don't even remember what the world looked like without it, because it has always been a part of your life.

> "IF YOU DON'T KNOW WHERE YOU'RE GOING, YOU MIGHT NOT GET THERE"
> (YOGI BERRA, WHEN YOU COME TO A FORK IN THE ROAD TAKE IT!: INSPIRATION AND WISDOM FROM ONE OF BASEBALL'S GREATEST HEROES).

So... how? How can you best handle this world of social media and technology? How can you engage with this stuff in a way that will keep you and everyone around you safe? How can you "learn to drive" the Internet in a way that honors yourself and other people and brings glory to God?

The first thing would be to recognize that this technology is a freedom — a gift, really — and not a right. If your parents are not cool with you being on social media sites yet, then that's cool. They know you better than anyone else, since they helped create you and have been raising you for the last 13 years or so. Trust their judgment and respect their boundaries if they don't think it's appropriate for you to start using these technologies yet.

Or maybe you're the one who knows you're not ready... and if that's you, I have all the respect in the world for you. I took my driver's test the moment I turned 16. My older brother was really different. He didn't see any rush to learn how to drive and didn't get his license until he was in college. There's nothing weird or wrong about admitting that you're not ready for the responsibility. There was no rush for my brother, and there doesn't need to be one for you, either.

But when you start engaging with this technology — not if, but when — please, learn how to drive it safely.

Social networking is great for things like sharing news, photos, funny or inspirational quotes, articles, blogs, and so on. It's an amazing way to stay connected to people you love, whether they live down the street or halfway across the country. It's definitely a big part of the high school experience, and I hope you'll find creative ways to engage with it to share information and connect with your friends.

It can also be an amazing way to learn more about your faith and share it with others. Pope Francis is on Twitter (@Pontifex), and he tweets all the time. I actually get his tweets sent directly to my phone as texts. It's awesome having his words pop up on my screen to encourage me in my faith. And since Rome is on the other side of the world, they usually come in the middle of the night. Many mornings, when I wake up, the first thing I see is an encouraging tweet from our Holy Father.

The good news is good across all kinds of media. I have tons of friends who Instagram artsy pictures with their favorite Bible verses typed over them, or who share sweet blogs and news about the Church on their Facebook pages. Jesus told us to spread the Gospel to all corners and peoples of the world, and Pope Benedict XVI once said that includes "the digital continent" — we need to talk about the Gospel online, too. We can and should share our faith *everywhere* we go, and that includes our social networks. And if you are bold enough to share your faith online, you'll be amazed at who you might reach.

But while there's so much good that can be done on social media... there are a lot of people using it badly, too. I don't want you to be one of those people, so let me give you a few tips I've picked up.

The first thing to remember is this: Once it's out there, it's out there, and you cannot take it back. Everything you text, tweet, snapchat, etc. — it all gets recorded somewhere and can be recovered. That's something I think a lot of us forget. We feel like if we delete it, it's gone. But it isn't. It's out there. *Forever.*

"I WANT TO DO EVERYTHING, EVEN THE SMALLEST THINGS, FOR THE GREATER GLORY OF GOD" (ST. DOMINIC SAVIO, SAINT COMPANIONS FOR EACH DAY).

I don't bring that up to scare you, but just to make you aware, because I think it's an important thing for you to know. We should always think carefully about what we post, and double-check our words and phrases to make sure we're saying exactly what we mean to say. Everything can be interpreted, and what you may think is funny or clever or innocent could be taken badly by someone else. So, before you click send, ask yourself a couple of questions: Are your words honoring and uplifting? Are your pictures beautiful and good? Are you engaging with technology in a way that respects yourself, others, and God?

> "IT IS A GREAT ADVANTAGE FOR US TO BE ABLE TO CONSULT SOMEONE WHO KNOWS US, SO THAT WE MAY LEARN TO KNOW OURSELVES" (ST. TERESA OF AVILA, *INTERIOR CASTLE*).

One great way to learn how to do this is to have an accountability partner, someone you can run things by. When I write a new tweet, I always ask myself if my boss or my mom would approve of it before I send it. Even when I'm just trying to be funny, I'll double-check. It's totally common for me to say my funny thought out loud to a friend before I tweet it (because then I know, based on whether or not they laugh at it, if it's actually funny or just funny to me).

And even if it is funny... one thing that I think so many of us forget is that just because we have a thought doesn't mean we have to share it. People who tweet 50 times an hour aren't showing off how clever they are — because *no one* is that clever that often. Does anyone really care that you had a ham sandwich for lunch and now you're watching TV (and live-tweeting the episode as you go) and you're going to clean your room later? Probably not.

Another reason it's good to have someone to run things by is because sometimes we might think or say something in the heat of an argument, for example, that we wish we could take back. Remember, there aren't any take-backs online. Think twice — even three or four or ten times — before possibly saying something that you might regret for a really, really long time.

So get in the habit of running things by other people, whenever you have any doubts about whether or not it's any good. Having outside eyes on our social media posts will help us learn to navigate those roads. Remember, one split-second of poor judgment could change everything.

Keep in mind, also, that once you put something out there (whether online or over texting), you have no control over where it goes. You may think that you're only sharing something — words or pictures — with certain people, but with a few clicks they can easily pass it on to whomever they want. Retweets and forwards and copied and pasted text messages can go viral in no time.

I once knew some teens who shared inappropriate pictures of themselves with one another, thinking it was their little secret, but one of them forwarded those pictures to some other students in their class. Then it was sent to some other people, and then the school found out and got involved. In an instant, they were both in big trouble and their reputations were seriously damaged.

You may encounter someone online or over texting who asks you to join in that kind of behavior — DON'T. First of all, it's incredibly disrespectful of someone to ask that of you. You're a person with dignity and worth, not a collection of body parts to put on display. If someone starts talking to you that way, do not be afraid to block or report them. And let your parents or another trusted adult know about it, immediately. There's no excuse for treating anyone that way.

Secondly, don't think that making mistakes in this area makes you a terrible person. Those two teens I mentioned above? They're really good people who had a split-second lapse in judgment. They apologized sincerely to their families and school. They faced

> "I SEE IN MY NEIGHBOR THE PERSON OF JESUS CHRIST" (ST. GERARD MAJELLA).

some consequences for their actions, including suspensions, but when they went back to school, their classmates forgave them. They learned a lot from their experience — and I hope you'll learn from them, too, rather than having to find all this out on your own. They really regret what happened and wish that they'd handled things differently — because, in some ways, their reputations (at least at their middle school) will never be the same.

Someone, much wiser than I, must have surely said this before, but it is so, so true: We are who we are when no one is watching. Are we proud of who we are behind closed doors? It's easy to put on our best behavior when we're around people we want to impress, right? Sometimes we all fall into that temptation of acting a certain way around one group of people (maybe family) and a totally different way around others (like our friends). Some of that is natural, just the different ways we relate to different people — but some of that behavior is fake. If we get in the great habit of being real, authentic people now (in real life and online), those habits will be with us for the rest of our lives.

It's sort of like Neville Longbottom from Harry Potter. In the final scenes of *Harry Potter and the Sorcerer's Stone*, when Harry, Ron, and Hermione were sneaking out of Gryffindor Tower late at night, Neville stood up to them — even though they were some of the smartest and coolest kids in the class — because he knew that what they were doing was wrong. And, because of that, in the end Professor Dumbledore rewarded Neville with ten extra points for Gryffindor — enough for them to win the House Cup. As Dumbledore said, "It takes a great deal of bravery to stand up to our enemies, but just as much to stand up to our friends."

Neville not only had courage, but he also had integrity. He knew the difference between right and wrong, and wasn't afraid to stand up for what was right, even if it would make his friends upset or compromise his chances at popularity. That's the kind of person Neville was, throughout the entire series. And (no spoilers, I promise) if you're a fan, you know that in the end, Neville played a *huge* role in defeating Voldemort forever — because he was a virtuous guy. He was intentional about becoming a good man, and doing what was right from the start. Isn't that the kind of person we all hope to be one day? Start now.

Those virtuous habits apply to our online lives, too. What we say matters, publicly and privately, because how we treat others is how we treat Jesus. Our faith teaches us that Christ is present in everyone we meet. In fact, Christ even says that whatever we do to others, we do to Him: "Amen, I say to you, whatever you did for one of these least brothers of mine, you did for Me" (Matthew 25:40). So how awful is it, then, that many teens become victims (and perpetrators) of online bullying? How sad is it that we have, so quickly, managed to turn these technologies against each other? Maybe it's just supposed to be a joke — or maybe someone really intends to be hateful — but whatever the reason, those actions are totally unacceptable.

Everyone has a right to a good reputation — that's why gossip is such a big deal, whether the words we speak about others are true or not. We know that rumors are damaging in real life. What makes us think they're any less hurtful online? They may even be more hurtful online because they can reach such a huge audience. Whatever we text, tweet, or comment about someone else we're saying about Jesus, since He lives in them. If our love for Him can be measured by our love for other people, then our words mean so much more than we really know.

One final caution about social media — because this is something even I struggle with — please don't let social media determine your worth. In the same way we can't be defined by our grades or extracurricular talents, we can't be defined by our social media interactions.

You might post a picture that gets a hundred likes or send a tweet that is retweeted all over the world. You also might post something that no one comments on. It doesn't matter. Our worth will never be determined by what others think or say about us. Whether something you've posted gets zero, one, or one thousand shares or favorites, it still has *nothing* to do with how good you are.

We all get caught up in that worry about what other people think of us, in real life and online. That's a normal part of being human, especially in high school. But no one else can determine our worth. To know how good we are, we must look to God. Saint John Paul II once said who we are is determined by "the sum of the Father's love for us and our real capacity to become the image of His Son" — we all have this awesome ability to look like Christ, because we are created in God's image and likeness. That's what determines our worth: How much God loves us, and how much we look like Christ in this world.

As more and more of your friends hop on social media sites, more and more people will "like" your stuff, but that will never determine your value. I know what it's like to post something I'm really proud of, and then feel disappointed when more people don't comment. I've even posted the exact same thing as one of my friends and noticed that my friend gets more "likes" than me. It's not a competition! And it has nothing to do with how smart, funny, attractive, or talented I am.

Sometimes, when I notice that this stuff is starting to get to me, I'll take a little break from it. I won't post or check on what others are posting as often — and it really helps. There are research studies coming out now that say people who ignore phone calls, social media alerts, and texts are happier overall. They have less anxiety and more chill-time. Don't be afraid to unplug! Not only will it help you to worry less about what others think about your posts, but it will also make you a better friend, classmate, sibling, and child.

> "I DON'T WANT EVERYONE TO LIKE ME; I SHOULD THINK LESS OF MYSELF IF SOME PEOPLE DID" (HENRY JAMES, *THE PORTRAIT OF A LADY*).

Nothing drives me crazier than when I'm out with a group of people and everyone is constantly checking their phones. Or there have been times where I see other people who are out with one another, and one member of the group spends the whole time texting. I know how easy it is to get in the habit of clicking your phone to check the time, and it's super handy to have Google there in case we can't think of the name of an actor or want to check the final score of a game that just happened — but seriously? Cut it out! The people who are sitting right in front of you are worth your time and attention.

In no way am I perfect at this — I'm actually super guilty. But I'm trying to get better. When I hang out with my next-door neighbor, I'll leave my phone at home. When I'm at a party or out to dinner, it stays in my coat pocket. We don't have to be 100 percent accessible to the rest of the world 100 percent of the time.

I'm not going to be offended if it takes someone a bit of time to respond to my call or text — I know my friends all have lives outside of texting me! Remember that your friends do, too, and don't worry if your phone goes silent for a little while. People managed to live thousands of years without cell phones, and they all made it just fine. Remember, this technology is not a right. It's a freedom and a gift. But the greater gift is actual face time with the people we love.

Love it or hate it, social media, texting, and cell phones are going to be a big part of your high school experience. Just remember that they don't define you. They're there to be used for good, not evil — and setting up healthy boundaries when it comes to technology is a great way to make sure that you use those things with integrity.

It's just like learning to drive... it's an incredible gift and a great freedom where a split-second decision could change everything. And as you learn how to engage with all these forms of technology, remember: You are who you are when no one else is around. Your words matter, online and in real life — because the way you treat others will always be the way you treat Christ.

PART // TWO
Relationships

// FOUR //

Relationship Status? It's Complicated: Family

Now that we've covered some of the how-to's of your daily high school life, like school and sports and social media, let's move on to another topic that will take up a lot of your time and energy: your relationships. And let's start with the people who you know (and who know you) best — your family.

Wouldn't it be great if your family were perfect? If "family" was that safe place you could come home to at the end of the day and just relax and totally be yourself? If everyone got along all the time and no one ever had a problem with anyone else? If you all sat together every night, snuggled up in your pajamas, huddled around a fireplace with cups of cocoa, singing your favorite Disney tunes in perfect three-part harmonies?

Yep... that'd be nice, all right.

I know my family doesn't work that way. We have it pretty good, actually — my mom, dad, older brother and I — but in no way has our family life been flawless. There was that one time, for example, when I thought I accidentally killed my brother.

We were having a fight, which was normal for us. We're only 14 months apart in age, so when we were kids, we really knew how to drive each other crazy. And when we were really little, we were the only friends we had. There weren't other brothers or sisters to hang out with, and our neighborhood was full of older couples — no kids. So when we got sick of each other, it's not like we had anywhere else to go.

One day, when we were probably six and seven, respectively, we were having an epic fight in the basement of our house. I couldn't even tell you what we were fighting over. I'm sure it wasn't anything important. But my brother came running at me to attack, so I grabbed the nearest weapon — a spray bottle of window cleaner — and held it out in front of me like a gun. He kept advancing, and I thought the safety-knob was twisted to the off position, so I decided to pull the trigger to try and scare him off. The handle was actually in the on position, which meant that I sprayed him good with bright blue cleaning liquid, right into his open mouth.

He stopped immediately and started crying, coughing, and spitting. His whole face turned red. I was sure I'd poisoned him — that window cleaner, after all, had a lime green toxic sticker on it, a sure sign that you don't want to drink the stuff. And I'd gotten my brother full in the face with it. We ran upstairs to our mom, who helped him wash out his mouth in the bathroom sink. He was crying because it tasted so bad, and I was crying because I thought I'd killed him.

Once we reached middle school, our relationship changed. We were old enough to have different interests and separate friend groups, so we did. And since we weren't hanging out with each other, we weren't fighting — something our parents really appreciated, I'm sure. We gave each other space in high school, too. He went to one of the all-boys schools, and I attended a Catholic co-ed. We had really different interests, schedules, and social lives, so we didn't spend much time together. We did both hang out at the same youth group — but even there, we were wrapped up in our own friends, our own hobbies, and our own lives. We went to different colleges, too. And now, as adults back in our hometown, we're the closest we've ever been, but we live in different parts of the city and don't see each other super often.

That's just a brief history of my relationship with my one brother. I can't even imagine how much more complicated a family gets when you add in more siblings...

We all know that no family is perfect. No two families are the same, and while some are great, others are difficult, and some are straight-up disasters — and again, none of them are perfect. My mom is the fourth of ten kids — five boys and five girls (and you can imagine how complicated it gets when you factor in their spouses, ex-spouses, and children). My dad had two parents and a brother, but they've all passed away, making him the only person still living from his immediate family. My immediate family is made up of my two parents (who have been married for almost 30 years), and my older brother, and now, a sister-in-law! It's so easy to see, from that small sample size, that every family looks different and comes with its own set of baggage.

> "You don't choose your family. They are God's gift to you, as you are to them" (Desmond Tutu, God Has a Dream).

There are divorced families, step-families, single-parent families, only children, 12 siblings, grandparents, aunts, uncles, cousins, and even those people who aren't technically blood relatives but you call them family — families come in all shapes and sizes. And as you get older, your family does too, which can mean a lot of changes for you and them. Families can face financial struggles, social issues, illnesses, deaths, abandonment, lying, cheating, or stealing… there are a lot of forces at work in the world trying to tear families apart.

You've got no say over what your family looks like. You can choose your friends, but you can't choose family. But you do get to choose how you relate to your mom, dad, brothers and sisters, grandparents and so on. That part is totally up to you.

> "The greatest gift that man can have this side of heaven is to be able to get along well with the people with whom he lives" (Bl. Egidio of Assisi).

For most middle schoolers, a lot still depends on their parents — and that's something that will continue for at least the first year of high school. You can't drive, and you aren't old enough to get any kind of regular job outside of babysitting or mowing lawns. Your parents still have a lot of say on how you spend your time and where you go to school and what extracurricular activities you're able to pursue. And it's their generosity that allows you to check out these different hobbies and interests, which is important to remember. Are you grateful to them for all the ways they support and encourage you?

You might have the opportunity to do more if you're an only child. Maybe you get involved in a certain sport or activity because it's something your parents or older siblings really enjoy. Maybe having a lot of siblings means less time and money for stuff like clubs and sports and more time spent babysitting your brothers and sisters. Maybe one of your grandparents is sick and living with your family as your parents try to take care of them and you at the same time. Maybe having multiple families means splitting time between two (or more) houses.

No matter what your family situation looks like, the only question I want you to think about right now is this: How can you be a better member of your family? Friends can be awesome, but friends come and go. Family is for life. And no matter how well (or how badly) things are going for your family, what part do you play in making your family the absolute best it can be?

> "YOU TOO TRY TO BRING THAT PRESENCE OF GOD IN YOUR FAMILY [...] LOVE BEGINS AT HOME, AND IT IS NOT HOW MUCH WE DO, BUT HOW MUCH LOVE WE PUT IN THE ACTION THAT WE DO"
> (BLESSED TERESA OF CALCUTTA).

When you start high school, you're going to get involved in a lot of new things. There's a new level of independence that comes with high school, right from the start. And that independence only gets bigger as you start driving, start working, and start making decisions about your future. But growing in independence does not and should not mean distancing yourself from your family. We are tempted to think that we don't need our families anymore, since we're more able to take care of our own stuff. But we do need them — we always will.

And one thing we're all going to need is more patience. Look, your parents are trying to figure all this out, too. They've never been the parents of a kid like you at the age you're at right now. Consider my brother and I, for example. We're just one year apart in age, but he's a boy and I'm a girl. And he's an introvert (more shy) and I'm an extrovert (more social). He's a really laid-back, chill dude, and I am a very strong-willed (that's putting it nicely) lady.

And those differences in our personalities? Those meant that when we were growing up, my brother was a piece of cake for my parents. He did pretty well in school, didn't get in a lot of trouble, enjoyed sports but wasn't obsessed with them, and was pretty easy-going overall. Me, on the other hand... well, let's just say it all started with a temper-tantrum about an outfit for family photo-day when I was four, and it never really stopped. Two kids, from the same parents

— but two very, very different people who needed different things from their parents.

The real story with your parents is that they just want to know you. That's a lot easier said than done, I know, but it's true. There isn't anyone in this world who cares more about you than they do, even if they don't always do a great job showing it.

> "To love a person means to see him as God intended him" (Fyodor Dostoyevsky).

It will probably annoy you, when your family starts asking you questions about your life, but please just know that they only do that because they care about you. They're actually interested in how your day went, what's happening at school, how things went at practice or rehearsal, what's going on with your friends. As you get older, and start heading in a million different directions, they'll have fewer and fewer opportunities to know what's going on with you. And the better they know you, the better they'll be able to relate to you. Please, don't shut them out.

I know that not every family has awesome, loving parents. Sometimes, for some families, the best thing is distance. Your parents or older siblings may have other issues going on in their lives that make it really difficult to relate to them. Sometimes our families need real help, and as teens, we can't do much about it. We don't have the knowledge or resources to handle some of those bigger issues. But even if that is your reality, know that your family is worth working on — even if the only thing you're able to do for them is pray.

> "Honor your father and mother, that your days may be long in the land which the Lord your God gives you" (Exodus 20:12).

A lot of times, our biggest hurts in life come from our families. If that's where you're at, I'm so, so sorry. Connect with a teacher or counselor or youth minister — some trusted adult — to get the help and healing you need. You're not expected to handle this on your own. I can guarantee, without even knowing you personally, that there are adults in your life who really care about your health and happiness, and if you come to them with any struggles or issues in your family life, they can help.

You play a really important, irreplaceable role in your family. You're the only person who can be you, for them. And you may be the best person to be Christ to them. When I was growing up, my family was Catholic, in the "we go to church every Sunday and send our kids to Catholic school and sometimes remember to pray before meals" sense. And when I was your age, graduating from eighth grade and heading into high school, I started to get really involved in my faith. I developed a relationship with God that was real.

And once I started going to youth group, my brother did, too. I didn't even invite him — he just decided to come with me one week, and then he kept coming. And because he kept coming, he got really into his faith, too. As a college student, he picked up a guitar and taught himself to play praise and worship music — and now, he's a professional music minister, and leads worship at three different Masses every weekend. Because my brother and I were both into our faith, our mom started going on different retreats and renewing her faith — and our dad, who had been away from church for a few years, started going back to Mass because my brother was leading the music.

> "LOVE ONE ANOTHER WITH MUTUAL AFFECTION; ANTICIPATE ONE ANOTHER IN SHOWING HONOR. DO NOT GROW SLACK IN ZEAL, BE FERVENT IN SPIRIT, SERVE THE LORD" (ROMANS 12:10-11).

You have no idea how badly God wants to use you in your family. And you also have no idea what kind of miracles He can accomplish through you, if you let Him.

Let's get practical for a minute: How might God want to use you in your family? What are some things you can do to love your family better?

First, pray. Pray for your family, pray with your family, and invite your family to pray more often. Secondly, make family time a priority. As things get more hectic in high school, you'll have less and less opportunities to hang out together at home. So schedule times when you all can hang out, and actually be present to one another (which means leaving the cell phone in your room). And when the members of your family have stuff going on — your little brother's baseball game, your older sister's dance recital — go and support one another. You appreciate it when they show up to your stuff, right? It means a lot to them when you come to their stuff, too.

Another great way to take care of one another is to help out around the house. If you unloaded the dishwasher without being asked... your parents wouldn't even know how to handle it. And it would be awesome. I'll challenge you to take it one step further — before logging on to Xbox, ask your parents if there's anything around the house they'd like you to do. Also, don't forget about your extended family. The reality is that grandparents won't be around forever, so take advantage of any time you can spend with them while you have them.

> "How good and how pleasant it is when brothers dwell together as one!" (Psalm 133:1).

You play such an important role in your family, and I'd hate for you to miss out on it because you're too busy texting your friends. I know how easy it is to hide in your room or spend every possible moment you can away from your house. I know that it's a lot easier to get over-involved in your favorite sports rather than diving into the lives of your siblings. I know that it's super annoying to answer the same questions every single day ("How was school today? Anything interesting happen? How are your classes? What's new with your friends?"). I know that some families can barely stand to be in the same room as one another.

But I also know, that if we're lucky, our families can be the greatest blessings we have. I can count on my dad to help me with anything. My mom is one of the first people I come to with my good news and with my problems. My brother is legitimately one of the funniest people I know — and one of my best friends, too. I was even a bridesmaid in his wedding. We've come a long, long way from me shooting him in the mouth with window cleaner.

As you start high school, one of the biggest decisions you will make is how to relate to your family. It's incredibly hard work to have strong family relationships, and may seem impossible at times, but I hope you'll try. You might be tempted to push your family away — high school is certainly an easy time to do that. But I hope you'll do your best to grow closer to them, because before you know it, you won't even live with them anymore.

We can't choose who they are, but we can choose how we treat them. And if we choose to love them (especially when it's difficult, and even when it hurts) then we can have the best possible version of family.

// FIVE //
Best Friends Forever?: Friendship

You may not be able to pick your family — but you do get to pick your friends. And man, you should be picky when it comes to your friends…

I ran through my memory and tried to count all the "best friends" I've had in my life and I think I counted 13. I'm not tying to show off how many amazing people have loved me — in fact, it probably makes it sound like my friendships haven't been especially deep. How can one person have so many "best friends" — doesn't that mean they weren't the best?

Some of them were the best, though, at the time. Some (not all) of those friendships were deep and great. None of them have been life-long, but at the point of life where they landed, they were exactly what I needed — and I hope that I was exactly what they needed, too. There have just been a lot of them because that is part of the nature of friendship. It doesn't necessarily last forever. A lot of our friendships are only in our lives for a short time, maybe even for a specific reason.

The friendship question is one of the biggest questions there is when it comes to moving forward into high school. When I talk to my freshmen friends, it's almost always their number one concern. Am I going to make friends when I get into high school? Are they going to be cool? Will they be a good influence? Will they get me into trouble? What about my old friends? Will we still talk to one another? Where will I fit in? What will I do on the weekends? How am I going to balance new friends and old friends at the same time?

Sometimes, that transition isn't so scary because we move on with a lot of the same kids we went to school with in junior high. I have friends who are from small towns where they went to the same school with the same kids from kindergarten all the way to senior year, whether they liked it or not. There are others of us, though, who leave a middle school full of people we've known for years and walk through the doors of a high school where we don't know a soul. That can be terrifying. It can also be super exciting.

So how do we hold on to the old friends we had? And how do we make new friends?

> "Friendship is born at that moment when one person says to another: 'What! You too? I thought that no one but myself'" (C.S. Lewis, *The Four Loves*).

Here's the thing about freshman year: *Everyone* is looking for somewhere to belong. You're not the only one trying to figure it out. And as time goes on, you'll get to know people better and will find those people who you naturally click with on a deeper level. That's where real friendship is found.

First, try not to worry about making new friends. I know that's so much easier said than done, but it's true. It won't do you any good to worry about it, anyway. The reality is that if you worry too much about making friends, you'll psych yourself out and become too nervous to be your awesome self — and being your awesome self is actually the best way to make friends.

How did you make the friends you have now? It probably started slowly... and it's okay if that's how it happens in high school, too. We've all been in this situation before: We're sitting in a classroom, waiting for class to begin, and someone makes a comment — maybe about the weather, maybe about the homework, maybe about the football game that's coming up next Friday night. Someone else responds, a conversation begins, and before we know it, we're making connections.

Jump into that conversation! Sometimes, we hold back, because we're afraid we might say the wrong thing or that people won't get it when we're trying to make a joke. I totally understand that fear... so say a prayer for courage, and open your mouth. Even if it's just to agree with something another person said, you've succeeded in putting yourself out there, and you'll be able to make connections with someone else.

I was absolutely terrified to start over at a new school in the middle of third grade. I was coming from the only school I'd known since kindergarten and walking into another school where everyone else had known each other since kindergarten. Everyone already had friends. No one was going to need or want me to join their group, right?

But from day one, there were two girls who were really nice to me, Annie and Carolyn. Even though the two of them were already best friends (and even though I heard the teacher tell them to let me tag along for the week), they were happy to include me — and I've always been grateful for their kindness. We didn't get super close because we didn't have much in common, but they were nice to me and saved me a seat in class. And those two things made a huge difference for me.

If you're the kid who is coming into high school with a solid group in place, please be on the lookout for that guy or girl who doesn't know anyone. There will almost certainly be at least one person like that in your freshman class, and he or she will be incredibly grateful for a seat at your lunch table during the first semester.

It doesn't necessarily mean you'll become "best friends forever" with that person. The same kind of thing happened when I started high school. I went from a Catholic grade school class of about 60 kids to a Catholic high school class of 180, and I think maybe seven or eight of my grade school classmates came with me. I spent the first couple weeks hanging out with my middle school friends, but as time went on, I got to know my new classmates better and made friends with the people I had stuff in common with — you know, more than just sharing the same junior high building. There's nothing wrong with letting those middle school friendships naturally fade, if you've both outgrown them. That's a normal part of life.

As time went on, whenever I joined a new club or activity, or went to a new youth group, or later when I started a new job... the same thing happened. I found people who laughed at the same jokes and loved the same kind of music. I'm not saying that I got along with everyone I met everywhere I went, but I always found someone

> "WE HAVE ALL KNOWN THE LONG LONELINESS AND WE HAVE LEARNED THAT THE ONLY SOLUTION IS LOVE AND THAT LOVE COMES WITH COMMUNITY" (DOROTHY DAY, *THE LONG LONELINESS*).

to talk to. That's why we talked so much about extracurricular activities in Chapter Two — because friendships come from common interests. By pursuing the activities you love, you'll meet people who enjoy the same things you do and find real friends. Remember, everyone is looking for friendship in high school. Be open to meeting new people, and you'll be amazed at how awesome some of the other kids in your school can be.

One caution, when it comes to making new friends in high school: There is going to be a huge temptation to latch on to the first group of friends who talk to you. I understand — it's a safe place to land. Have you ever heard the saying "any port in a storm"? We get scared of the storms and desperately look to stop at the first place that looks safe. But the first group of kids who talk to you when you walk in the door for freshman orientation may not necessarily be the best kids for you to hang out with.

My friend Dominic had to make that kind of decision before high school actually started. He was making the transition from a small Catholic grade school to a large public high school and was, honestly, a little nervous about it. As he hopped on the bus for freshman orientation, a couple of guys started talking to him and asked him if he smoked weed. He didn't, and said so. The kid responded by saying, "Well, if you ever want to try it out, you can come smoke with us." Dominic replied with a polite but super clear "thanks, but no thanks; that isn't my thing" — and that was it. From day one, those kids (and anyone else on the bus who was listening) knew what kind of guy Dominic was.

> "WALK WITH THE WISE AND YOU BECOME WISE, BUT THE COMPANION OF FOOLS FARES BADLY" (PROVERBS 13:20).

That's the key — Dominic knew who he was and was confident enough in that moment to let those guys know, too. High school is a huge time of growth, where we make a lot of decisions that shape us into the people we're going to become. And if you're like Dominic — knowing enough about who you are to know what road you want to take in high school — you've got a huge advantage when it comes to making good friends.

It's pretty simple: We look like our friends. The people you choose to hang out with are going to have a huge influence on how you spend your time, and how you spend your time has a lot to do with what kind of person you will become. In that moment, Dominic made a decision that he wasn't going to join up with these guys — not because they're terrible guys, but because they were into harmful stuff that could seriously mess up their lives. It's an excellent game plan to stay far, far away from people like that because of the huge potential they have to change your life for the worse. Choose your friends very, very carefully.

> "Do not be led astray: 'Bad company corrupts good morals'" (1 Corinthians 15:33).

When Jesus was running around the planet 2,000 years ago He had hundreds (if not thousands) of people who followed Him and spent time hanging around. But He chose the twelve apostles very carefully. The twelve definitely weren't the coolest, most popular, most successful guys around — but they were the right guys for the job. They were the guys with the right heart, the right passion, and a real love for the Lord. So Jesus picked them to be His closest companions.

You should be kind to everyone, obviously. Dominic didn't start yelling at the guys who offered him weed. But it's a great idea to be selective about your close friends. You can and should love everyone in a Christ-like way, but don't feel guilty about picking your closest group of friends very carefully. The first people you talk to when you walk in the door may not be the right guys for the job — and there's nothing wrong with recognizing that.

And as you're busy making these new friends in high school, what's going to happen to your friends from your old school? If you have great, faithful friends from junior high in your life, do whatever you can to keep those friendships strong. Good friends aren't measured by popularity, rude jokes, or demanding personalities. A good friend is loyal, kind, selfless, and fun to hang out with. A good friend is someone who loves you for who you are. We all need those people in our lives who really care about us, but don't think we're the best thing that's ever happened, right? Because those are the people who will speak truth to us and help us to be the best people we can be.

> "No one has greater love than this to lay down one's life for one's friends. You are My friends if you do what I command you" (John 15:13-14).

My friend Paul had that in junior high, and let it go. He had a good buddy named Karl who was a faithful friend — the kind of friend who would ride his bike a couple of miles to Paul's house so they could hang out. He was kind of a quiet dude and his clothes weren't the most stylish, so when the guys got to high school, there were other boys in the class who thought that Karl was a big loser. So Paul stopped hanging out with Karl, even though he was a much better friend than these other guys that Paul was worried about impressing. And now, looking back, Paul has huge regrets that he ditched a legit friend because he was too worried about what some other people thought.

Sometimes our friendships end because we're like Paul, trying to get in with a group that we think is cool. There's a huge difference between that (which is totally uncool) and friendships naturally fading away (which happens). Do you know what I mean? Nothing bad happens, we just don't talk or hang out as much as we used to. I had a couple of grade school friends that I kept in touch with after graduation, especially during freshman and sophomore years of high school. But as time went on and things changed and people changed, we saw each other less often. We didn't have any kind of serious falling out — no major fights or mean girls stuff — but that kind of thing happens over time, and that's okay.

There's no need to feel guilty if those friendships end. God uses those people to meet us where we're at, and as we grow and change, our relationships will change, too. A lot of people spend a lot of time and energy clinging to old friendships that have naturally faded, which leads to a lot of hurt feelings and anxiety. Don't go there. If it's time to move forward and let those relationships go (whether that's your doing, or someone else's), then it's time. Thank God for the time you had, and keep your eyes open for what comes next.

It happened with my high school friends, and even some of my college friends. Remember the 13 "best friends" I mentioned at the beginning of the chapter? Some of those people are still in my life, and some aren't. And none of us are losing sleep over it.

But you know which people have really stuck? My oldest, longest, strongest friendships are all with people I met in youth group as a high school student. Sister Mary Mother of Truth, for example: we met on a retreat at the end of eighth grade (her name was Claire, back then), and we got to be really close friends as high school sophomores, contemplated being college roommates and then, when we didn't end up at the same school, we made sure to visit each other several times a year. She is, without a doubt, one of the best friends of my life. And I know she always will be.

Now that she's a religious sister, she lives in another part of the country with her order, and she comes home twice a year. When she's home, she's home and we hang. We spend so much quality time together — we catch up on everything that's been going on. Her last home visit was nine days long, and I saw her or talked to her every single day she was here!

But when she isn't home... we don't have that kind of communication, and that's okay, too. We actually don't talk at all — and it's not because we can't. It's because we're both pretty bad at long-distance communicating. Whoops. It's not like she has a cell phone I can text whenever I want, you know?

But that's OK, too, because we have something even better. We see each other every day — in prayer. Whenever I go to Mass, I know she's there, too. She has to be, because it's a part of her life as a religious sister. I know that she went first thing in the morning when she woke up; so on those days when I go, too, I meet her in the Eucharist.

Have you ever heard of the Communion of Saints? It's a really cool teaching that all the faithful on earth, in heaven and in Purgatory are all united through God — which means that every time I go to Mass, I go with Sr. Truth. If she's at Mass and I'm at Mass, then even when we're in different cities, we're at Mass together.

I know that sounds super spiritual — maybe even a little weird, right? But it's true. Because she and I both have a strong relationship with the Lord, on our own, we meet each other there, in Him. And our strong relationship with God keeps our friendship strong, too. When we were teenagers at youth group together, even though we went to different high schools, we'd see each other at prayer group and Mass and on retreats. That made the time we spent together on Friday and Saturday nights even more legit, because we knew what was *really* going on in one another's lives.

I'm not saying that you or your best friends have to become religious brothers or sisters if you want to keep in touch after high school (although that would be sweet). But, in my own life, I've found that friendships based on something real are friendships that last. And there's nothing more real in this world than our faith in the One who created it all. Those friendships will (hopefully) outlast this world and carry on into the next.

My friends from high school and I bonded over our classes, our favorite movies and TV shows, and things that were happening at school. We weren't fake with one another, but our common interests were kind of shallow things. Those things aren't bad things, but they definitely don't last. But my friends from youth group and I bonded over our faith, our hopes and dreams for our lives, and our pursuit of a strong relationship with God. And on top of all that, they're *fun*. I always laugh the hardest when I spend time with them.

If you know who you are and what you really want out of high school, then you will find those kinds of friends. I hope that you'll be like Dominic, and avoid the temptation to link up with the first people who talk to you when you can see that those people aren't going down a good path. I hope you won't be like Paul, who ditched a legit friend because someone "cooler" thought that guy was a loser. And I hope you'll find friends like Sr. Truth (back when she was Claire), who are chasing after God with their lives and will help you run after Him, too.

"THERE IS NO MORE PRECIOUS EXPERIENCE IN LIFE THAN FRIENDSHIP" (ELEANOR ROOSEVELT, BOOK OF COMMON SENSE ETIQUETTE).

Your friendships are naturally going to bloom and fade with time — that's a normal part of life. And our friends help determine who we will become, so be picky. Surround yourself with people who love you and will speak truth to you. Look for those people who bring out the very best in you.

That's how you get friendships that really do last forever — for this life, and hopefully, for the life to come.

// SIX //
The First Time I Fell In Love: God

All of our relationships are in our lives for a reason. There's so much we learn from being in relationships with other people. Your family is your first community, the people who teach you about life and love. And your friends — well, they teach you about loyalty and fun. And hanging out with people who have different personalities can bring out different parts of our own personality, and help us to be more well-rounded people.

There's a reason we thrive in community, a reason we worry about and work on our relationships. It's because we were made to exist in relationship, with one another... and with God.

If you're a graduated eighth grader and you've picked up this book, for whatever reason, chances are good that you are what we lovingly call a "cradle Catholic." You've probably been Catholic your whole life, right? Baptized as a baby, Mass on Sunday with the family, maybe you went to Catholic school or spent one night a week up at church for religious education. Sound familiar?

I don't know about you, but I don't know a lot of 14-year-old converts. You probably didn't choose to be Catholic. It was chosen for you.

I've been Catholic my whole life, too. I was baptized as an infant and lived in one of those families where we went to Mass every Sunday, no questions asked. My brother and I went to Catholic grade school and high school. We made our First Reconciliation and First Holy Communion in second grade, and were Confirmed as seventh graders.

And when I was in your shoes, getting ready to graduate from eighth grade and take that next step into high school, if you had asked me who Jesus was, I probably would have told you that He was like a character in a story.

It's a really good story, right? There's a teenage virgin and she gets pregnant, but it's okay, because it's God... as a baby. And His name is Jesus. He grows up in a small town where He learns to be a carpenter from His adopted dad, Joseph, and as an adult He starts teaching and preaching. He works a few miracles and gains some followers, but there's one group of people who really didn't like Him, so they work together to get Him arrested and killed. He goes through this really brutal, gory death on a cross, but it's okay, don't worry, because three days later He rises from the dead because (don't forget) He's also God.

Lots of crazy characters and interesting plot twists? Absolutely. But to me... it was just a story. So if that's where you're at with Jesus, I get it. I know it's easy to think of Him the same way we think of George Washington or Abraham Lincoln. He is someone we study, someone we learn about in school. And church? Well, lots of people go to church. It's just another building where we spend an hour once a week, if that.

We know that Jesus was a real guy, who really lived and died, and was important in history... but what does that have to do with us?

That God stuff was important to my mom, and my teacher, and my priest, but it wasn't really that important to me. I believed in God, for sure, and prayed to Him like Santa Claus when I wanted or needed something, either for myself or for someone I loved. Sometimes I paid attention at Mass, but usually it was pretty boring. And in religion class, it was easy to let my mind wander because we talked about the same stuff over and over again, every year. I already knew the story. I didn't need to hear it again.

Then, at the end of my eighth grade year, it all changed for me. I had these two friends who were going to spend a weekend on a retreat at a nearby parish. It was a retreat just for eighth graders graduating and getting ready to move into high school, and they were both really excited about it. One of them, Sarah, was going because her older sister was a teen in the youth group and wanted Sarah to come with a bunch of friends. The other, Nikki, had been going to this parish's youth Mass for a while and loved the guitars and drums and homilies that were focused a little more on the teens.

> "WE KNOW THAT ALL THINGS WORK FOR GOOD FOR THOSE WHO LOVE GOD, WHO ARE CALLED ACCORDING TO HIS PURPOSE" (ROMANS 8:28).

But I didn't really want to go on this retreat. I'd been on a day-long retreat as a seventh grader, preparing for Confirmation, and I thought it had been pretty boring. So why would I want to give up a whole weekend for more of that? But the more Nikki and Sarah insisted, the less I was able to argue, so I signed up to go. We even managed to recruit our friend Lorrie, too.

So, the four of us made our way down the road to another parish to spend a weekend on this eighth grade retreat. Outside of each other and Sarah's older sister, I didn't know a single person there. There was a youth minister running the show and high school students who had volunteered to be there to give talks and lead us in our small groups. And every single kid from the eighth grade class at that school had come as a participant — so that made the four of us feel even more awkward. There were talks, and skits, and games, and music… it was all okay, I guess. Honestly, it just seemed like more of the same boring activities as that seventh grade retreat I'd been on.

Then, on Saturday night, everything changed.

They took us down to the church and had us spread out in the pews on one side. The youth minister talked for a really long time, and to be honest, I barely remember a word he said. But something really stood out to me because I had never heard it before. He said that when Jesus was on the cross, my face flashed across His mind.

I'd been Catholic my whole life and had never heard that before: When Jesus was on the cross, your face flashed across His mind.

Then the youth minister said we were going to do an activity, and don't be afraid, no one was going to hurt us (which immediately made me afraid — why would you say that unless there was a chance that I was going to get hurt?!). And as we sat in the pews, the high school students came and selected four or five of us at a time, randomly, to go through the activity. I was in the very last group to go. I just had to sit, and wait, and wonder, as I watched the other kids disappear down a back stairwell and come back up on the other side of church.

Finally, someone tapped my shoulder and led me down the stairs. At the bottom of the candlelit stairwell, I walked through the Stations of the Cross — as if I were Jesus. Instead of just hearing the story, I was walking through that moment. I carried the wood, I touched the nails, I heard the hammering and whispers of "All hail, the King of the Jews," and "We don't want You, we want Barabbas."

And the whole time that I was going through this activity... I was still just telling the story in my head. It wasn't anything shocking or new. I already knew the story, because I'd been hearing it my entire life.

When it was over, they led me back up to the church with the other retreatants and sat me in a pew by myself. And as I sat there, I thought. For the first time in my life, I really thought about this person, Jesus. I thought about the activity I had just walked through — and the crucifixion He had actually endured — and about the fact that when Jesus was on the cross, my face flashed across His mind.

And then the musician played a song that I had never heard before. He sang about Christ on the cross and the physical pain Jesus experienced on that day. But the crown of thorns on His head, the spear that pierced His side... that physical pain was nothing compared to the heartache He felt for each one of us. And He still feels that ache, today, for us to be with Him. That song included an invitation, near the end. It asked if I would open my heart to Christ standing before me and say yes to His amazing love for me.

And I burst into tears. Seriously loud, embarrassing, ugly-cry tears. I still don't have the words to explain what happened to me in that church on that night, but I just knew, in a way I had never known anything before and in a way I have never known anything since, that Jesus is real. He's not just a character in a story, but a real person, who really lived and really died in a horrible way — ten thousand times worse than the stations I had just walked through.

And that while He was going through all of that, He was thinking of me. My face flashed across His mind.

And He was thinking of you. And He hasn't stopped thinking of you for a moment since then. He can't get you out of His head. If He stopped thinking of you for a moment, you would cease to exist.

That moment was a huge moment of conversion for me, even though I'd been Catholic my whole life. I had to make a decision: if Jesus was real, then my life would have to look different. He had given up everything, for me. He had suffered so much, out of love for me. And not only had He done all of that, then, but He rose from the dead and lives now. And He wants nothing more than to have a relationship with me. He feels the same way about you.

So I decided, right then and there, that I would work on having that relationship with Him. I regularly attended youth group, spending more and more time with those people who wanted to know Jesus more, too. I started actually paying attention at Mass (I don't know if you've ever tried that; I know I never had before) and praying on my own. I began learning more about the Church and going on retreats… I just wanted to know Him. And the more I got to know Him, the more I fell in love with Him. I fell in love with my faith, too.

It's not like you and I have two different options here. Right now, you're being faced with the same decision. Because Christ went through all of that for you, too — so it's time for you to answer the question of who He is and what He will mean to you.

"If we let Christ into our lives, we lose nothing, nothing, absolutely nothing of what makes life free, beautiful, and great [...] Only in this friendship are the doors of life opened wide" (Pope Benedict XVI).

Because as much as He was thinking of me, and as badly as He wanted a relationship with me… He wants all of that, and more, for you.

Diving into my faith changed everything about who I became in high school. It determined the way I spent my weekends, who my best friends were, how I treated my classmates, the way I interacted with my family, the way I dated, the clubs and activities I pursued, how hard I worked in school… everything! And I know that every aspect of my high school experience was better because of it.

What kind of high school experience are you looking to have? One with depth, joy, peace, and freedom? Done. He's got that for you. Because I made my faith a part of everything I did, I know it made everything I did the best it could possibly be. In high school I had amazing friends, a really good relationship with my family, an awesome dating relationship, and a lot of fun on the weekends and over the summers — all because I chose Him, first, at the very end of my eighth grade year.

He will do the same for you. Nothing would make Him happier than to walk through the next four years of your life (and beyond) alongside you.

> "Draw near to God and He will draw near to you" (James 4:8).

It wasn't my parents, or my teachers, or my priest that chose Him for me, just like I can't choose Him for you. It was my decision. I wanted Him in my life. My faith shaped me into the person I am today, and I'm so, so grateful.

I'm not saying that believing in Him makes everything perfect. We all know that's not true. The world is a crazy, messed up place, and bad stuff happens to all of us, whether we believe in God or not. But having that relationship with Him makes handling all that other stuff so much easier, because we know that it all means something. And He can bring good out of any bad situation.

If you're in that place, where Jesus is just a character in a story... trust me, I totally understand. I've been there and I know what it's like to not care — at all — about your faith. Maybe you've never had an experience of Him that has made Him real to you. Or maybe you don't live in a place where faith is important to anyone around you, so how could it be important to you? Maybe you've grown up in the Catholic Church and it's just something that's always been a part of you life, not something you've ever chosen. And maybe it's been super boring. Trust me, I get that, too.

But I also know that none of that has anything to do with whether or not Jesus is real. He's real if our families love Him or not. He's real if our church is boring or not. He's real if our friends think He's lame or not. He's real if we pray or not. There isn't anything we can do or say that will change the reality that Jesus is God and He wants to be with us more than anything else in this world.

The only real question is whether or not we will choose to be with Him.

Jesus was a real-life historical figure, just like George Washington and Abraham Lincoln. That much has been proven. But the biggest question we all face is whether He was just a guy, or God.

If you're in that place, where He's just a guy, then I'm going to beg you, right now, to learn more. Learn more about the Faith and spend time in prayer. Take advantage of the sacraments, especially Reconciliation and Eucharist — two of the most tangible ways our God comes to us on earth. We can't have a relationship with someone we never spend time with, so meet Him in the sacraments, in prayer, and in Scripture.

It's okay to go into those things not fully understanding what's happening. If we waited to go to God until we had it all figured out, we'd never get there. He's too big. But we can all start moving towards Him, and as we seek to know Him and learn more about our faith, our relationship with Him will grow.

> "At every time and in every place, God draws close to man. He calls man to seek Him, to know Him, to love Him with all his strength (CCC 1).

Don't worry if you have questions about the Church and Her teachings, either. I hope you do! Asking questions is one of the ways our faith becomes real to us. If we never ask any questions and just accept everything at face value, our faith will be shallow and easily shattered by the first person we meet who asks us a question that we cannot answer.

Just do me a favor: Direct your questions to solid, holy, smart Catholic people. If I wanted to learn about zoo animals, I wouldn't ask a construction worker. That's not his area of expertise. In the same way, when we want to learn more about our faith, we should go to people who know the faith. If I ask an atheist about Jesus, what exactly do you think he's going to tell me? He'll probably spend his time trying to convince me that all this Jesus stuff is nonsense. But that person's beliefs don't change the fact that Jesus is real — so if I want to learn more about Him, I should talk to someone who knows Him.

And if you're already on fire in your faith — if you've had great experiences of Him or just love prayer and the Church — that's awesome! Don't stop learning! Keep chasing after the Lord and growing in your relationship with Him. I promise you won't regret it. If I had stopped with that first retreat, my relationship with Him wouldn't be very meaningful. In fact, it would only be based on my feelings — I'd think that when I "feel" like God is near, He is, and when I don't, He isn't. That couldn't be further from the truth. God is always chasing after us, whether we're "feeling it" or not.

The more we chase after Him, the more we realize how real and amazing He actually is. We're never going to know everything about Him, and as we grow and change, there will be ways that our relationship with Him grows and changes. There will be times when we need Him to be our best friend who sits with us, our Dad who carries and comforts us, our teacher who leads us, a true love who romances us… and He can and will be all of those things for us, and more. He will never get boring. I promise.

> "To be saints is not a privilege for the few, but a vocation for everyone" (Pope Francis).

There are so many amazing ways that God wants to work in your life. But this is your relationship with God that we're talking about here, and only you can decide what that means. I can't choose Him for you (although I absolutely would if I could). You have to.

If you've decided against Him — if God is like Santa Claus, just for little kids; if church is boring and a waste of time; if there's no way all this Jesus stuff could be real when life has been so hurtful — please, please reconsider. He already knows who you are, whether you believe in Him or not. But He doesn't just want to stalk you, He wants to know you. A relationship with you is the most important thing to Him. He can't wait to get to know you better.

If we open our hearts and minds to having a relationship with Him, I know that He'll surprise us. He did it to me, in eighth grade. And He hasn't stopped surprising me yet. He'll do it for you, too.

And if you're not sure about Him… that's okay. There's no reason for you to expect to have it all figured out by the time you walk into high school. That's what a lot of high school is for. Just do me one favor: Don't stay in that place of "maybe He is, maybe He's not." Take the necessary steps to learn more. At the very least, make a decision that you'll give all this God stuff a chance. Try out youth group. Go to lunch with your parish priest. Spend time talking with a youth minister or campus minister. Read a book. Read the Bible.

Pop into the church and sit for ten minutes. Saint John Paul II said that it doesn't matter *how* you pray *as long as* you do pray. So pray — and keep learning more.

The reason I insist that you do something about this is that when it comes to the question of Jesus (Is He real? Does He matter?), there are three possible answers but only two places to land. You can answer with yes, no, or maybe... but at the end of the day, maybe always defaults to no.

"FOR PRAYER IS NOTHING ELSE THAN BEING ON TERMS OF FRIENDSHIP WITH GOD" (ST. TERESA OF AVILA).

If your answer to Jesus is, "Yes, You are real and I want to know You," then keep going. He has so much in store for you. If your answer is no, I beg you to reconsider. Go on a journey where you get to know Him better. You've got plenty of time and resources to help you along the way.

And if your answer is maybe... then go on that journey, too. But make sure that you're moving. You can sit on that "maybe" as long as you like, but you won't get anywhere with it. If a friend invites me to come to a party, and I accept, he knows I'll be there. If I say no, he knows I won't. But if I say maybe, then when the evening of the party comes... if I haven't decided to change my maybe to a yes, I'm not going. A maybe always defaults to no. God is too important to answer with a maybe — and I don't want you to land on "no" just because you never moved from "maybe."

He's a really big deal... because He's real. And choosing whether or not to follow Him is the biggest decision you will make in your life.

"OUR HEARTS WERE MADE FOR YOU, O LORD, AND THEY ARE RESTLESS UNTIL THEY REST IN YOU" (ST. AUGUSTINE).

So why not start now? If you want high school to be the best it can be, then don't go through it alone. Go through it with Him.

PART // THREE
Chastity

// SEVEN //
What does that word even mean?! : Introduction

I have a couple questions for you. Are you interested in having great relationships? The last section was all about your relationships, with family, friends, and God. Would you like all of those relationships to be better? How about a relationship with someone who is cute, maybe has a little potential, you know what I'm saying? Great! What about respect — would you like to be respected by members of the opposite sex? Have them treat you kindly and just generally be cool around you?

Well, I know a great way to get both of those things — great relationships with everyone in your life and respect from everyone around you. I'll give you a hint. It's through a virtue that I really love. In fact, I'm kind of obsessed with it. It's called chastity.

"Chastity is the sure way to happiness" (Saint John Paul II, Love and Responsibility).

I've heard a lot of different people give a lot of different talks about chastity, which can be kind of overwhelming. So to make sure we're on the same page, let's start with my favorite definition of chastity: Chastity is a virtue (which means a habit of doing the good) that is all about respect. That's it. It's so simple, actually — chastity simply means a habit of respect.

It's about respect for yourself, for your family, for your friends, and for someone who is cute and has a little potential (you know what I'm saying). It's about respect for your future spouse, if you get married some day, and your future children, if you have kids one day. It's about respect for everybody in your world because it's simply about respect for sex itself.

So, someone who is living the virtue of chastity says, "Look, I recognize that sex is a good thing. So I'm going to save sex (and all sexual acts) for marriage; and if I get married one day, I'm going to keep those things within my marriage."

But there's a little more to it than that, right? Because, even though we all know that sex is physical (*duh*), chastity is about so much more than just purity of our bodies. I'm not just a body, and neither are you. We all have bodies, hearts, minds, and souls, and chastity is about purity in all of those areas. It's about purity of our whole selves.

That's a totally amazing thing, because we live in a world that can be pretty messed up when it comes to this stuff — love, sex, dating, and relationships. If you look around at our culture, you can tell that many people aren't in this habit of respect. So many songs, movies, and TV shows treat sex like it's a joke. A lot of people think sex is no big deal. Everyone's all, "Oh, she's just being Miley," right?

But because I live the virtue of chastity in my own life, I know that sex is a really big deal. It's sacred, holy, and good. And even though I live in this world that gets it totally wrong, that doesn't mean that I can't listen to the radio or go see a movie. It means that I can tell the difference between God's plan for our sexuality versus the lies that our world tells us about sex and relationships.

Chastity is about the way we talk, the way we joke around, the clothes we wear, the thoughts we have. It's about being respectful with our whole selves and not treating ourselves (or anyone else) like anything less than a total person — someone with a body, heart, mind, and soul that deserves real love and respect... even if that person doesn't know how to respect himself or herself.

Another thing about chastity that's so great is that it's a lifelong virtue. It's for all vocations. That means that if you get married one day, chastity is for you. If you become a priest or a nun one day, chastity is for you. If you are #foreveralone, chastity is for you. It's for *everybody*.

And the greatest thing about chastity being a lifelong virtue is that you can start living it now (today!), and live it for the rest of your life. The sooner we make a decision to choose chastity, the easier it will be for us to live out that virtue.

The first time I ever heard about chastity was in seventh grade, when someone gave a talk to my class and told us that God wants us to save sex for marriage. I thought that sounded like a pretty good idea, so I made a commitment to do my best to live out the virtue. Then, as a high school student, I learned that chastity is about so much more than not having sex outside of marriage — it's about the way we live our whole lives, that habit of respect. I thought that sounded like an even better idea. And I'm so glad that I committed to chastity before I ever started dating, because it was a lot easier to be chaste in my dating relationships since I'd been growing in the virtue of chastity since I was 13.

> "A CLEAN HEART IS A FREE HEART"
> (BLESSED TERESA OF CALCUTTA).

Another thing that's so cool about chastity is that it is not about the past. Chastity is about the present and the future. So, if we've made mistakes in the past, it doesn't matter. We can start living chastity today, and live it for the rest of our lives (remember, it's a lifelong virtue). It doesn't matter where we've been, what we've done, what we've said or seen or worn... none of that matters because chastity is about the present and the future. Jesus says, in the Scriptures, "Behold, I make all things new." That's me, and you. It's all of us. He can help us start over and commit to living a life of chastity.

Chastity is such an amazing virtue because it's one of the ways we live out our commitment to Christ. It's how we keep Jesus at the center of our relationships — and you said you wanted great relationships, right? Let me give you a hint: If you want your relationships to be the best that they can be, you better have Jesus at the center of them, because He is the source of all life and all love. Chastity is also an amazing way to say "yes" to God with our bodies, hearts, minds, and souls.

Being in that habit of respect helps us to truly love one another. Chastity isn't about saying "no" to sex. It's about saying "yes" to God's plan for our lives and His amazing design for our sexuality.

> "THIS IS THE WILL OF GOD, YOUR HOLINESS: THAT YOU REFRAIN FROM IMMORALITY"
> (1 THESSALONIANS 4:3).

One of the things God did, when He invented sex, is that He designed it for two purposes: babies (that's where babies come from, in case no one ever told you...) and bonding. Sex creates a really strong bond between two people, which is a really great thing for marriage. I don't know if you've ever been married before; I haven't, but I hear it's tough, and having that strong bond helps keep a married couple together in good times and bad.

But that bond gets created any time two people have sex, whether they're married or not. And outside of marriage, that bond can be really damaging and cause a lot of pain. It can keep couples together who aren't actually a good match — if they've taken their relationship to a physical level, it's really difficult to stay away from one another, because the bond that's been created is so strong. It can cause a lot of jealousy and suspicion, making people really possessive of one another. When it leads to rumors and gossip around school, it can devastate someone's reputation and their own self-esteem.

And when that bond is broken, hearts get seriously broken, too. It can be like a mini-divorce — we've all seen how painful a divorce can be, and when two people have a broken sexual relationship, they go through a lot of the same feelings that a divorcing couple goes through, even though they weren't married. They're breaking a bond that God never meant to be broken, and the results are really, really painful.

But chastity saves us from all of those negatives, and frees us up to have the positives instead. When chastity is at the center of our relationships, we know that when someone wants to date us (if they've chosen chastity as well), it's because they actually like us — they aren't trying to get something from us, or feel better about themselves, or prove anything to their buddies. They are genuinely interested in who we are... they think we're cute, smart, funny, interesting, and they just want to know more about that. And another way chastity helps boost our confidence? We know that we don't need to be in a relationship to feel good about who we are. Our worth doesn't come from having a boyfriend or a girlfriend. Our worth comes from God, and nothing can mess with that.

We also have the freedom to end bad relationships without the heartbreak of a broken sexual bond. And when we are in chaste dating relationships, we know we can trust the people we date because they're also in that habit of respect. No matter where they're at or who they're with, we know they're being respectful. And when we do find someone to marry, if God calls us to marriage one day, we know that our bond with our spouse will be incredibly strong. If we're both committed to living the virtue of chastity, then we've been in that habit of loving and respecting each other for years — and we're ready to love and respect each other for the rest of our lives.

So, how? How do we live out this commitment to chastity?

The first step is to be bold. If you make a decision to live chastity, then let people know about it. I'm not saying that when you walk into a party and are meeting a bunch of people for the first time that you have to be all, "Hi, my name is Rachel and I love chastity!" as you shake their hands (although, I guess you could, if you wanted — but that might be awkward, especially if your name isn't Rachel). But, if you do make a decision to live chastity, then definitely let your family, your friends, and any people you date (or are interested in dating) know that you are committed to this virtue. It's a lot easier to live chastity when you have people in your life supporting you and backing you up as you try to grow in this habit of respect.

That might sound a little weird… going on a date with someone for the first time, and looking at them and saying, "You know, I'm really excited that we're going on this date, and I just wanted to let you know that I'm committed to living chastity and saving sex for marriage." It's okay, if that sounds a little awkward to you — but realize that it might mean that you're not ready to date yet, and that's okay, too. We'll talk about that more in the next chapter…

> "I ask you, instead, to be revolutionaries; I ask you to swim against the tide. Yes, I am asking you to rebel against this culture that sees everything as temporary and that ultimately believes you are incapable of responsibility, that believes you are incapable of true love" (Pope Francis).

Being bold in living this virtue is going to look different for all of us, because we're all different people, but there are some things that will work for most of us. I really recommend having some kind of reminder that you've made a commitment to chastity. Many people sign chastity commitment cards (like I did, in seventh grade; and I look forward to giving it to my future husband one day, to show him how long I've been waiting for him). I've known people who keep those cards in their wallets, on bulletin boards, in their lockers... some place where they see it often and it reminds them of the commitment they've made to chastity. Some teens I know have even been really bold and posted pictures of their signed chastity cards on all of their social media accounts — letting everyone know that they've made a decision for chastity. Other people wear a ring or maybe a saint's medal on a necklace. Whenever they see these signs of their commitment, they're reminded to keep working on living this virtue.

One way we can all be bold in living out the virtue of chastity is to embrace modesty. So many people struggle with the concept of dressing modestly — it just doesn't sound *cool*. And what's the big deal, anyway? Everyone else is dressed that way, right?

The big deal is that lust is a sin — just like gossip, judgment, and envy are sins. The way we dress can lead other people into all of these sins, and we're responsible for the effect we have on others. someone is dressed immodestly, it sends a very clear message of, "I don't care about respecting you, or myself." Chastity is that habit of respect. That includes the way we dress — and the way we look at others.

> "WHOEVER CAUSES ONE OF THESE LITTLE ONES WHO BELIEVE IN ME TO SIN, IT WOULD BE BETTER FOR HIM TO HAVE A GREAT MILLSTONE HUNG AROUND HIS NECK AND TO BE DROWNED IN THE DEPTHS OF SEA" (MATTHEW 18:6).

I know people who say, "Look, I should be able to wear whatever I want. It's no big deal." But it is a big deal. It hurts women, who look at one another and constantly make comparisons (such as "I could never look that good in that," or even "Oh my gosh, she should *not* be wearing that!") and it creates a huge temptation for men, to look at women as a collection of body parts, rather than a whole person. Remember, we aren't just bodies — we're bodies, hearts, minds, and souls. And dressing modestly helps others to see us that way, as whole persons.

Practically speaking, what does that look like? It means passing on clothes that are too tight, too short, too low-cut, too sheer... things that are too much but not enough, all at the same time. Leggings, yoga pants, and other super-tight exercise clothes are too revealing to be worn with anything other than a longer, looser top. And it's called underwear for a reason, everybody… it was made to go under our other clothes. The only person who should see it is you (and whoever does your laundry).

I know modesty doesn't sound very bold… but it is. There are ways to embrace what's stylish without disrespecting ourselves or anyone else. When we live the virtue of chastity, we act with respect for ourselves and for everyone around us through the way we dress. It *is* bold. And it's good.

> "Many live like angels in the middle of the world. You, why not you?" (St. Josemaría Escrivá).

Another way chastity calls us to be bold is in the way we speak. It's been a struggle for me, hanging out with friends who tell inappropriate jokes or talk about members of the opposite sex in a way that's disrespectful. Be bold enough to not join in those conversations, and if you're really bold… stop them. Change the subject, maybe even call people out (as lovingly as possible, of course), and help them move forward. I'm not saying you have to get all preachy, but it's possible that they don't know anything about chastity, and you could be the person who shares it with them.

My other big tip for living chastity is to be prepared. When you find yourself in a situation where you might be tempted to break chastity, know ahead of time how you're going to handle that situation. When you start going on dates, have a plan for the date — know what you're going to do, where you're going to go, and whom you're going to be with. And when you're surfing channels or browsing online, and find something you know you shouldn't look at, have a plan to turn it off immediately. When someone speaks to you disrespectfully, either in person or over texting or on another kind of social media, know what you'll say in response to tell them to stop, and block them if necessary.

> "Let no one have contempt for your youth, but set an example for those who believe, in speech, conduct, love, faith, and purity" (1 Timothy 4:12).

It's a lot easier to make the right decision in the moment, if we've already made that decision *before* we're in that moment. This is true of our sexuality and the virtue of chastity, but it's true of a lot of other virtues, too. It's so helpful when it comes to making friends, talking about others, knowing how we're going to act at parties, etc.

Decide who you're going to be, and do it on purpose; otherwise, you might fall into some temptations that you will really regret later.

And my final tip on living chastity is to not be afraid. Don't be afraid to let people know you're living chastity. Don't be afraid to stand up for yourself and your beliefs when it comes to chastity. Don't be afraid to get yourself out of an uncomfortable situation — like texting your parents and asking them to pick you up early from a party, even if you were planning on spending the night. You deserve to be treated with respect every moment of your life, and anyone who cannot treat you that way does not deserve to be in your presence.

> "Only the chaste man and the chaste woman are capable of true love" (Saint John Paul II, Love and Responsibility).

I know that chastity is a difficult virtue to live, but it is so incredibly worth it. Chastity helps us to get the best out of all our relationships — family, friends, romantic, and otherwise. We can give — and receive — real love and respect in all of our relationships with other people.

Chastity helps us to have the very best. And you were created for the best... please, don't settle for anything less.

// EIGHT //
Don't Waste Your First Kiss: Dating

Have you had your first kiss yet? I kind of hope you haven't — not because I'm anti-kissing (in fact, I'm a huge fan of it), but because I've heard a lot of stories about middle school kisses being less than spectacular. They're almost always awkward, too. Maybe not as awkward as what happened to my friend Pete, but I'll let you be the judge of that...

It was the summer between seventh and eighth grade, and Pete was hanging out with his buddies at the pool (because everyone who was anyone from his middle school spent their entire summer at the neighborhood pool). The whole class was hanging around, but split up, naturally — the boys on one side and the girls on the other. That day, all the boys were gathered around Pete and all the girls were gathered around Katie.

Katie was easily the most beautiful girl in the class. And because she was so beautiful, all of the guys were way too afraid to ask her out — all the guys except Pete. He figured that since no one else would do it, why not? If she said no, it wasn't like she had said yes to anyone else before. And since no one else had asked her out before, when Pete came over and asked her if she wanted to go out, she said, "Sure, why not?"

The fact that Katie and Pete were dating didn't seem to change much. The boys still hung out on one side of the pool, and the girls on the other. But now, all the boys were gathered around Pete, "The Guy Who Katie Said Yes To," to talk about how awesome it was that Katie was going out with him.

And all they really wanted to know was whether or not Katie was a good kisser.

When they asked him about it, Pete kind of laughed. "I... I, uh, I don't actually know."

The guys couldn't believe it. "What? You haven't kissed her yet?!" "Dude! You've got to kiss her!" "I can't believe you haven't kissed her yet!" "Yeah, man, go kiss her!"

So, Pete, high on confidence from the fact that he was "The Guy Who Katie Said Yes To," walked boldly over to the girls' side of the pool and asked Katie if she would take a walk with him over to the tennis courts so that they could talk. All the girls giggled, and Katie said, "Sure, why not?"

They went over to the tennis courts together, not talking, as the boys watched from one side of the pool and the girls watched from the other. Pete laid out his towel and they sat down together.

"So, the guys have been asking me if we've kissed yet."

"Yeah? The girls have been asking me, too."

"Yeah? Well... I guess we should kiss, then."

"Sure, why not?"

And then, in Pete's own words: "So we drooled on each others' chins for about five seconds and it was over. I went back to the boys, and she went back to the girls, and when school started again, we broke up."

Romantic, right? Sure, why not?

My first kiss was a little different. I didn't date anyone in middle school — not because I didn't want to date anyone, but because none of the guys really wanted to date me. But during my sophomore year of high school, this really great guy who had been one of my best friends for about a year asked me out. I said yes, of course, and we dated for about a month before he kissed me for the first time.

It was a Friday night — it was Good Friday, actually (you know the day that Jesus died? I made out... So my friends and I started calling it "Gooooooood Friday"). We had been to the services at our church, and stopped by the grocery store to get some ice cream to eat after midnight, when the Good Friday fast ended. We went back to my house, and watched a little TV with my family, ate our ice cream after midnight, and when I walked him to the door at the end of the night, we stopped on my front porch and he kissed me goodnight.

It was so perfect — soft, sweet, not too short or too long. And there weren't any spectators or drool anywhere in sight.

In some places, the pressure to date in middle school is ridiculous. It's crazy, right? Boys and girls used to be total opposites, gross even, and now they suddenly look a little more interesting... And when they start to pair off, I know that it can be tough to be left behind on that. It would be totally awesome if someone that you liked also thought that you were cute, funny, smart, and interesting — but let me ask you a question: Would you rather have the tennis courts or the front porch?

Please, don't waste your first kiss.

If you've already had it, I hope it wasn't wasted. I hope it was with someone that you really liked and were actually interested in having a relationship with. But I'm smart enough to know that isn't usually the case in middle school. The tennis court scene seems pretty standard.

So if that's how things went for you in middle school, I hope you don't waste your second kiss. Or your third. Or any other kisses you have over the course of your life.

Don't get me wrong, I wanted the tennis court scene, too (although at my school, it would have been at the end-of-the-year carnival). But I didn't get it in middle school, and what I did get, near the end of my sophomore year of high school, was so much better. And even though I had to wait 16 years to get it, I'm so glad I did.

"LET LOVE BE SINCERE"
(ROMANS 12:9).

There is no reason to be in a rush to start dating. You are not half of a person if you don't have a boyfriend or a girlfriend — you're a whole person, on your own! You've got plenty of cool things going on in your life already — school, sports, family, friends, other hobbies, and interests. You don't need someone else to complete you or make you whole. Nothing is missing, I promise. I know so many incredible, healthy, well-adjusted, good-looking people who choose not to date until after high school (some until after college) because they're just too busy being awesome on their own.

High school is an amazing part of life where you get to focus on being you and doing the things that you like — don't take this the wrong way, but it really can be all about you. And when you start dating, there are a lot of things that you'll have to make about the other person. Their activities, their friends, their families will all become a part of your life. That can be a really cool thing — but it is definitely not something you need for the first day of freshman year. There's a lot of freedom in being able to figure out high school without the added pressure of having someone else's heart in your hands.

I know that even as I say "don't be in a rush to start dating," some of you are replying, "too late." Okay, that's cool too. If you're already dating someone, then make sure you date them right. The virtue of chastity must be at the center of your relationship — remember, that habit of respect, saving sex and all sexual things for marriage? There's a whole chapter about the virtue right before this one. Flip back for a refresher as often as necessary. If chastity isn't at the center of your relationship, then your relationship cannot possibly be all the awesome things that God wants it to be.

Dating relationships exist to help us learn how to love and respect other people, as we figure out God's plan for our vocation... if He's calling us to marriage, the priesthood, religious life, single life, whichever. Chances are pretty good that you aren't going to marry the person you date in high school. And the reality is that most of our relationships are going to end, right? Ideally only one will last forever — the one person that we marry, if we get married one day. Chastity helps us to keep that in perspective and treat the people we date with respect as we learn more about ourselves and who God has created us to be.

Whether you've already begun dating or not, there are a few key steps that need to be in place before you really dive into any relationship. The first thing is to choose chastity. Learn more about the virtue and make sure you understand what it really means to live it — Chapter 7 has hopefully given you a good start. Living chastity on your own (with the way you think, dress, speak, etc.) will help you get in that good habit of respect and will really prepare you for living it within a relationship, whenever you do start dating.

Second, talk with your parents about dating. If you want to start dating before you start driving, then your parents have to be cool with it because they are your main method of transportation. But more than that, it's a respect thing. Your parents love you more than you'll ever know, even if they aren't always good at showing it. And they certainly have some ideas about what it might look like for you to be in a relationship with someone.

I know some parents who have clear rules about dating — no dating until high school, no dating until 16, group dates are okay but not one-on-one, curfews, etc. You should definitely talk with your parents about their expectations *before* you enter into a relationship. See what they think about dating in high school, and talk to them about what you want out of your relationships. Let them know that you're committed to chastity, and ask for their help in living it.

There's nothing embarrassing about making a decision for holiness, and by letting your parents know that's the kind of kid you are, not only will they trust you more, but they can also help you live that out in your dating relationships. And if having that conversation sounds awkward — you know, if saying, "Hey, mom and dad, I'm committed to chastity and saving sex for marriage!" sounds tougher than saying, "Hey, mom and dad, I don't really want to talk about my romantic relationships with you" — then that's a pretty good sign that you're not ready to date. If you can't talk about your relationships with your parents, it sounds like they aren't relationships you should be in. And those kinds of relationships don't end well.

Then, talk about chastity with the person you're dating — make sure he or she has chosen it, too, because it's also a lot easier to live it when you are both on the same page. It's really important for you to sit down with a person you think is cute and let them know that you're choosing to be chaste in the way you date. You should both have clear boundaries for what is and isn't acceptable, physically, in a relationship (and I'd recommend keeping it at kissing, as a maximum, because anything beyond a simple kiss will probably tempt you to do more).

It's also a great idea to have that conversation before you even kiss for the first time, to help you figure out whether or not you and this person should even be together. By talking about this stuff at the beginning, you'll be able to tell, right away, if the two of you are on the same page when it comes to chastity. Your words can help you figure that out — and knowing where the other person stands on chastity will help you figure out whether the two of you are capable of having a good relationship.

That might sound kind of awkward, right? If it does, then that's a sign that you're not ready to start dating, and that's okay too. Remember, there's no rush. But you have to be able to have that conversation with someone you're dating — over and over again throughout your relationship — to make sure that the two of you want the same things. If you can't even talk about chastity, you'll have a harder time living out chastity and your relationships will not be the best that they can be.

> "Do not awaken or stir up love until it is ready"
> (Song of Songs 2:7).

Next, be smart about the way that you date. Have a plan for your dates — know where you're going to go and whom you're going to be with. The most essential part of dating is getting to know someone, and some places are better for that than others. Remember what I said last chapter, about how "being prepared" is one of my top tips on how to live chastity? That definitely means having a plan for your dates, because let's be honest: There are some things that you might be tempted to do, at home alone, in your parents' basement, "watching a movie," that you just aren't going to do out in public. It'd be super uncomfortable. You'd probably get arrested...

So take your date out somewhere — anywhere, even if it's to a Denny's or an IHOP because those are the only places open in your town past 10:00 p.m. It's a much better idea to have your alone time in a public place — that's the kind of set-up that will lead you to your ultimate goal: happiness and freedom in your relationships. If the key part of dating someone is getting to know them, then what better place is there to have a conversation than some funky, old Denny's? There's nothing that's going to tempt you to violate chastity while you sit across from one other in a vinyl booth, drinking bad coffee while 1980s power ballads play softly in the background.

You will be much happier with the decisions you make there, rather than in the basement...

And get creative! I don't know what it's like where you live, but where I'm from, there are so many awesome (and often free) things to do. Take advantage of the events your city has to offer — parks, festivals, fun shops, restaurants, whatever. Even if you live in a smaller town where there doesn't seem to be much going on, there are tons of fun dating activities that you can set up on your own. Bake cookies together, map out a scavenger hunt, play games or sports together — there are tons of options, when you really think about it.

Sometimes you just need to think outside the box. Dinner and a movie is a fine date, but when you just give it a little extra thought, you can come up with something truly great. My friend Luke once picked up a date right after school and took her to a park, where they painted pumpkins for Halloween and made peanut-butter-covered-pinecone bird feeders for the trees. Then, he laid out a giant role of bubble wrap and played dance music through his car stereo so they could have an outdoor bubble-popping dance party. Finally, he took her to a nice restaurant for dinner and brought her home early enough that she could still get her homework done. She said it was the best date that she had ever been on.

That kind of date is worth waiting for. I know the temptation is to go with the first person who seems interested, but really, what's the rush? Don't waste your time on someone who doesn't really respect or care about you. Dating can be an awesome part of the high school experience — but it doesn't have to be.

You might feel ready to date... and find that no one seems ready to go out with you. I've been there, too, my friend. It isn't easy. There have been plenty of times where I had my eye on a guy who wouldn't have seen me if I'd been covered in sirens and lights with a giant arrow pointing at my heart.

"There's no need to be dismayed if love sometimes follows tortuous ways. Grace has the power to make straight the paths of human love" (Saint John Paul II, Love and Responsibility).

But remember, your worth doesn't come from your relationships, but from God — one of the great benefits we get by choosing the virtue of chastity. You'll have the rest of your life to be in a relationship with someone, if God calls you to marriage one day. There's no rule that says you must have a boyfriend or girlfriend every second of high school in order to get there.

Whether you date in high school or not, just make sure that you date well. Please don't waste your first kiss — or any of your kisses, in fact. Make them count.

You get to choose: the tennis courts or the front porch? Some things are worth waiting for, I promise.

// NINE //

Media Savvy: Purity of Mind

Have you ever met someone with a super-devotion to a team, or a band, or a celebrity?

You know the type, I'm sure. That one guy who will rearrange his schedule around his favorite sports team, who has all the stats memorized, whose fantasy league is the center of his social life? Or the girl whose social media profiles all feature the word "Bieber" and you can't see the paint on her bedroom walls behind all the boy-band posters? What about the fans who reread their favorite book series once a year, spend hours watching YouTube videos about the latest scoop on the developing movie or television deal for the story, and show up to movie premieres dressed as their favorite character?

We all have that tendency to become huge fans (or outright psychos) over our favorite bands, TV shows, actors, and movie series. We buy every song, watch every episode, spend hours online researching, and drop tons of cash on their merchandise. (I know it sounds crazy, but it's actually totally normal. I'll give you a hint: We act this way because God wired us for worship. He made us this way so that we'd worship Him. We're just really, really good at directing that worship to other places…)

And even when we don't seek out pop culture, it's always around us, isn't it? You don't even have to go looking for it, thanks to the wonderful world of advertising. There once was a day when YouTube didn't come with commercials... can you imagine? Ads flash across websites, promoted tweets invade our Twitter timelines, and even Instagram comes with sponsored photos these days. It's never-ending.

I read an article recently that said that today's teenager spends an average of eight to 11 hours a day consuming media (meaning music, movies, TV shows, video games, social media, etc.). EVERY DAY. Seriously?! Eleven hours a day is a lot of time. Is that even as much time as you spend sleeping? I wish I got 11 hours of sleep every night...

And we all know that a lot of the media we consume is not exactly a ringing endorsement for the virtue of chastity. Every funny movie makes jokes about sex, or pornography, or birth control, or strippers. Dramas on television usually include people sleeping around, even cheating on their spouses. The lyrics of most pop songs make it sound like partying and having sex is the only way to enjoy life. And our favorite performers are constantly looking for ways to shock and surprise us... but how surprising is it, really, to have a half-dressed woman shaking her booty on a stage?

> "Since love cannot be sold, it is invariably killed by money" (Jean-Jacque Rousseau).

It isn't news that sex sells. And here's a heads-up: That's exactly why it's all over our media. Our entertainment industry knows that sex is the key to getting our money, as a culture, and that's the name of their game. Advertising agencies and movie and music producers have one bottom line: the cash inside your wallet. They don't really care about the state of your soul.

It's not their job to keep your heart pure. They're not concerned with how their messages affect your heart, mind, or soul, or the how ways that they portray sex, love, or dating impact your relationships. It's their job to keep your piggy bank empty because you've spent all your money on their product. I'm not saying they're outright evil people (I couldn't, because I don't know their hearts). I'm just saying they have a job to do and they're really, really good at it.

And the fact of the matter is that everything we consume has the possibility of becoming a part of who we are. You've heard that phrase, "You are what you eat," right? That's true physically, with food. It's also true mentally and spiritually, with media. If we just mindlessly watch television or listen to the radio without thinking about the messages we're taking in, then those lies about sex and our sexuality ("sex is no big deal"; "everyone is doing it"; "sex leads to love") will become a part of who we are — they'll contaminate our hearts. All those impurities in the media will penetrate our hearts and change the way we think about sexuality.

But a pure heart is one that can tell the difference between the truth and the lies. Jesus said it, in the Beatitudes — "Blessed are the clean of heart, for they will see God" (Matthew 5:8). When our hearts are clouded by sin or lies, we miss out on the Truth. Sex shouldn't be the center of our lives, like the media makes it out to be. Love should. That's God's greatest desire for all of us — to love and be loved, by Him and by everyone else around us.

If I asked you to think of some unchaste messages you've seen in the media lately, I'm sure it wouldn't take you long to come up with a lengthy list. Off the top of my head, I can think of everyone from pop singers to fast food restaurants who will use sex (either as a joke, or as pornography) to keep us interested.

> "My strength is as the strength of ten, because my heart is pure" (Alfred Lord Tennyson, "Sir Galahad").

Because of course we're interested, right? Our sexual desire and sexual curiosity is a normal, healthy, natural thing. God created it within us. Sexuality is a huge part of being human and we should never be ashamed of it. But there's an important difference between having our sexual desires under control and letting our sexual desires control us. If we buy into the lie that sex should be the center of our lives, it will change the way we see ourselves and other people. We stop seeing others as people to be loved and begin looking at them as objects to be used for our own pleasure. But when we have our sexual desires under control, we have the freedom to look at people as people. We're free to truly love them — to work for their good, not just our own.

I know the world says that freedom is doing whatever you want to do, whenever you want to do it. But Jesus calls Himself the Truth that will set us free — and says that anyone who sins becomes a

> "To be chaste means to love with an *undivided* heart. The unchaste person is torn and not free. Someone who loves authentically is free, strong, and good"
> (*YouCat* 406).

slave to sin (John 8). You've probably experienced that on some level — ever struggled with a sin that looks like a really bad habit, like gossip or cussing? Those sins are hard to break because we just get in that habit of committing them. The same thing can happen with sexual sins because our sexual urges are incredibly strong. If we don't keep them in check, they can easily take over. Chastity helps us grow in self-control and keeps us free from slavery to our sexual desires. That's one of the most amazing benefits of chastity — it brings us real freedom.

And the way that our culture uses sex to sell us products has enslaved so many people. It turns human beings with dignity and worth into a collection of body parts. We're constantly bombarded with lies about our appearances, the meaning of sex, what's normal and healthy and good in a relationship, and so on. People should be loved and objects should be used, not the other way around.

So how do we keep our minds pure in a world that loves the fact that sex sells? My first piece of advice is to start calling it out. Work on a mental filter. When you're watching a movie, pay attention to the relationships and the way sex is a part of the storyline. Is it just a big joke? Is it happening casually outside of marriage? Or is it justified because the two characters are in love? Call it out — all those scenarios are unacceptable. What about when you listen to the radio? There are lots of catchy pop songs out there that have lyrics that make it seem like sex is no big deal. Call it out — sex is a big deal; it's really important and it's sacred. Recognize that the message you're hearing is garbage, even if the singer is talented or the beat is catchy. Call it out — that message isn't in line with your beliefs.

> "A clean heart create for me, God; renew within me a steadfast spirit"
> (Psalm 51:12).

I live in the same world you do, and I love movies, TV shows, and music. I'm not saying that living the virtue of chastity — doing our best to keep our bodies, hearts, minds, and soul pure — means we can't watch a movie or surf the Internet. It just means that we must consume all media critically — and we have to keep calling it out. Rather than just letting the messages of the media wash over us and running the risk of letting those lies become a part of who we are ("You are what you eat," remember?), we look at everything very carefully. We have our filters in place and can tell the difference between truth and lies. We hold on to what is good, and reject what's bad.

Developing this kind of filter is not an easy process. I hope you've got people in your life who will help you build one up. When my friend Andrea was growing up, as one of four daughters in the house, it was a pretty common occurrence for her and her sisters to sit down and watch a romantic comedy (or straight-up sappy "chick flick") with their mother. And every time there would be a love scene with two characters who weren't married to one another, Andrea's mom would grab the remote, pause the movie, and say, "What's wrong with this picture?" And all the girls would say, together, "They're not married" — usually accompanied by a pretty serious eye roll.

Andrea thought it was kind of annoying, at the time — she just wanted to watch the movie, after all. But now, Andrea is so glad that her mom helped her to get a solid filter in place, because as a teenager who was dating, she knew that sex was made for marriage and it helped her to keep her standards high when it came to relationships. Now, she's happily married to an awesome guy who also loves chastity. Her mom's movie commentary is actually a big part of her own "happily ever after."

And speaking of happily ever after... There's a story I love about an ancient bishop named Nonnus who lived in Antioch in the fifth century. Legend has it that he was walking down the street with a young priest when they passed a young woman, named Pelagia, who was dressed pretty scandalously and was probably a prostitute. The young priest immediately turned his eyes away because he didn't want to sin by lusting after this woman. But Bishop Nonnus couldn't help but look at her in the eyes, with tears in his own eyes over such a beautiful soul leading such a messed up life.

So which guy did the right thing? Well... both of them. The young priest knew himself well enough to know that he needed to avoid what the Church calls the "near occasion of sin." He wouldn't be able to look at that woman purely, so he turned his eyes away in order to avoid treating her disrespectfully, as an object. And the bishop knew himself well enough to know that his heart and mind were strong in chastity and he'd be able to look at the woman with love, in the eyes, as a daughter of God.

And because of his love, she was converted. Now, all three of them are saints.

> "YOU HAVE HEARD THAT IT WAS SAID, 'YOU SHALL NOT COMMIT ADULTERY.' BUT I SAY TO YOU, EVERYONE WHO LOOKS AT A WOMAN WITH LUST HAS ALREADY COMMITTED ADULTERY WITH HER IN HIS HEART" (MATTHEW 5:27-28).

When we have a solid filter in place, we can watch a movie that makes jokes about sex and know that they aren't truly funny, but laugh at other parts that are actually clever and good. We can recognize that the lyrics of a particular Miley Cyrus song are powerful, beautiful, and true — and pray that her vocal talent, not the way she uses her body, will sell records in the future. In the meantime, we can skip buying those records because we don't support artists who don't respect themselves. We can walk through a shopping mall and turn our eyes away from the ads that use sex to sell, choosing instead to buy clothes from shops that don't turn people into objects.

There's no shame in looking away. It's actually a great idea to take media breaks and detox from all the trash that's out there in our world. We don't have to be plugged in 24/7 — we'll be much better off if we aren't. We should have a balance in our lives — 11 hours per day is too much time to spend on almost any one thing. We've all got school, sports, clubs, family, friends, and our faith to focus on, too. So put down the phone and shut off the computer once in awhile. It might sound crazy, but it's actually good for your mental health, I promise. Plus, it'll give you more time to pray... and we could all use more time to pray.

> "HOW CAN THE YOUNG KEEP HIS WAY WITHOUT FAULT? ONLY BY OBSERVING YOUR WORDS" (PSALM 119:9).

By periodically stepping away from media, we'll remove ourselves from a lot of temptations. Looking away is one of the best things we can do for our own hearts, minds, and souls. Because we live in a world that says that sex is no big deal, pornography is considered normal. Some people even say it's healthy and good — but please, please, do NOT buy into that lie. People don't talk about it enough, but viewing pornography is one of the easiest ways to distort the true meaning of sex and our sexuality.

Sex was created for two reasons, remember? Babies and bonding. But pornography twists the true meaning of sex and our sexuality, and turns something beautiful into something awful. It treats people as objects to be used for our pleasure and makes something sacred into something less than ordinary — something vulgar and gross. Back in the day, people had to go looking for pornography, but now we live in a world where, sadly, porn comes looking for us. It's everywhere, instantly, with the way our technology works. And it's a terrible idea to engage with it.

Saint John Paul II once said that the problem with pornography isn't that it shows too much of people, but rather too little. It separates bodies from souls and causes us to look at human beings like animals. And often, the acts depicted in pornography are perverse — not things that normal, healthy people do. It's also ruining our relationships with one another (because it horribly affects the way men and women see each other) and it's a highly addictive behavior, actually rewiring the chemicals in our brains.

> "I AM NOT FIGHTING A HOPELESS FIGHT. PEOPLE WHO HAVE FOUGHT IN REAL FIGHTS DON'T, AS A RULE"
> (G.K. Chesterton, *The Flying Inn*).

If pornography is an issue for you, please, do whatever it takes to get help. I've known teens (guys and girls) who have found freedom from that addiction and are in much happier, healthier places now. They told their parents, even though it was awkward, and found friends to hold them accountable, and made regular use of the Sacraments of Reconciliation and the Eucharist so that God's grace and mercy could help them on their way. One of the ways the devil can keep us enslaved in our sin is by making us think we're in it alone, which has the effect of keeping it secret and preventing us from getting the help we need. Don't let this have a secret power over you.

Do whatever you need to do to keep yourself free from pornography. Immediately shut it down if it ever pops up on your computer or phone. If it's a real temptation for you, keep your electronic devices in a public space in your house where you won't be tempted to go there. Lean on the sacraments and prayer, especially the prayers of our Mama Mary, to give you strength and help keep you pure.

> "Purity is the fruit of prayer" (Blessed Teresa of Calcutta).

God can and will help us have pure hearts, no matter where we've been in the past. Remember, chastity isn't about the past — it's about the present and the future. So even if we've made mistakes, it will be OK. Talk to God about it, because His mercy is new every day (Lamentations 3:22-23).

You're an amazing person — more than just a body. You're a body, a heart, a mind, and a soul. And as a whole person, chastity will bring you freedom to really love and respect everyone in your world — even people in the media who can't love and respect themselves.

Our culture is straight up crazy when it comes to sex. Some people are motivated by love of money, some out of loneliness, and some out of a distorted desire for authentic love. But chastity helps us to tell the difference between the truth of God's love and His design for our sex lives, and the lies of our culture that tell us how to get those things we really want.

Jesus said to worry about the stuff within, because that's what will ruin us on the outside (Matthew 15; Mark 7). Purity of your heart and mind is difficult, but doable. It will take some practice and a serious commitment to chastity. So start working on that filter now, before you step foot into your high school. It will make all the difference for your relationships once you get there.

// EPILOGUE //

Don't Worry About High School — Jesus Doesn't.

My favorite thing about being Catholic is the fact that we have a God who knows exactly how we feel. That's the awesome advantage of the Incarnation (God made man): He has been where we've been and felt what we've felt. He is exactly like us in all things (except sin — Hebrews 4:15).

He knows what it's like to be nervous, excited, scared, confident, worried, happy, stressed out, lonely, goofy — dare I even say, awkward? It couldn't have been easy being the only sinless kid on the playground, after all. No matter what we go through, He understands. He knows how we feel, because He's been there before.

That's true of high school, too. Yeah, I know — Jesus of Nazareth, in the flesh, is not going to walk down your hallways, carrying a stack of books and trying to not trip on His robe as He shuffles from class to class. But because our God became one of us, He will be there beside you. His Holy Spirit lives within you, through your Baptism, and He is always, always, always with you. He also knows exactly what you're about to face, and trust me when I say that, He isn't worried about any of it.

He's been through all the struggles, triumphs, and temptations that will come for you once you arrive. Everything, good and bad, that comes with high school? Jesus knows how to handle it. He can navigate school, sports, clubs, family, friends, dating, chastity — all of it. He's got it under control.

And He has everything you need to make it out of high school alive. He came to bring us life, after all, and life to the fullest (John 10:10). Jesus doesn't just want you to survive high school… He wants you to love it. He wants you to spend the next four years growing, more and more, into the incredible person that He has created you to be.

Not only that, but He wants to go through it with you. One of my favorite names for Jesus (you probably hear it a lot around His birthday) is Emmanuel — God with us. That's His number one priority: simply being with us. He wants to walk with you, side by side, through all the craziness that comes with high school and beyond.

And if you decide to walk through high school with Him by your side, then everything will be a lot easier to handle. The best decision of my life was to follow Jesus at the end of my eighth grade year. I met Him on a retreat, I knew He was real, and I decided to seek Him with my whole heart. And because I made my relationship with Him my number one priority, my high school years were amazing.

They weren't perfect — I fought with friends, I struggled with learning how to balance new responsibilities, I lost loved ones, I had crushes on people who didn't like me back, I felt awkward and ugly and insecure and lonely at times. It happens. I'm human.

But so was Jesus. It's an amazing gift to know that the all-powerful God of the universe knows what it's like to be a person on earth. He shares our humanity, and He walks with us through it all.

As a high school student, I faced all of the same temptations you're about to experience. Some of them didn't faze me, because I knew my identity as a child of God and was confident in the decisions I made. The devil's biggest lie (think back to Adam and Eve in Genesis) is that God could somehow hold out on us — as if there's any good thing in this world that God doesn't want us to have. So the devil sets sin before us and tries to convince us that it will make us happy.

But because of my relationship with God, I knew that real happiness was found in Him and no temptation could ever bring me joy. I wasn't perfect, by any stretch of the imagination (and I'm not now). Sometimes I fell, and whenever I fall, God picks me back up through the sacraments and I start again.

And all of that began when I was sitting in your place, graduating from eighth grade and getting ready to set foot inside my high school. I shared all my joys, fears, nerves, and frustrations with Him, and as I put my life into God's hands, He showed me the right path to walk. He gives me the strength to keep going, even when I'm tempted to give up or give in.

Whether you're thrilled, terrified, nervous, or pumped about going into high school (or all of the above), I don't want you to be worried. Because Jesus has been where you've been. He knows exactly how you're feeling and He will be right by your side, whatever may come your way.

This book has some ideas on how to be Catholic in high school — and I hope that they've been helpful ideas to you — but when it comes down to it, the main point is simply to be with God. If you choose to go into high school with Him by your side, He will give you everything you need to make it the best four years it can be.

Your high school has no idea what's about to hit them, through you. So be His, stay close to Him, do whatever you can to keep growing in your relationship with Him... and go get 'em.

LifeTeen.com